SAY IT IN
JAPANESE

Revised and Enlarged Edi...

by

DOVER PUBLICATIONS, INC.
New York

The Dover *Say It* series is prepared under the editorial supervision of R. A. Sorenson.

Published in Canada by General Publishing Company, Ltd., 30 Lesmill Road, Don Mills, Toronto, Ontario.
Published in the United Kingdom by Constable and Company, Ltd.

This Dover edition, first published in 1983, is a completely revised and enlarged work, which supersedes the book of the same title originally published by Dover Publications, Inc., in 1954.

Manufactured in the United States of America
Dover Publications, Inc.
31 East 2nd Street
Mineola, N.Y. 11501

Library of Congress Cataloging in Publication Data

Kai, Miwa.
Say it in Japanese.

(Dover "say it" series)
Includes index.
1. Japanese language—Conversation and phrase books
—English.   I. Title.   II. Series.
PL539.K24 1983   495.6'83421   83-8999
ISBN 0-486-20807-9

CONTENTS

iv CONTENTS

INTRODUCTION

Japanese is the language of over 117 million people in the main Japanese islands and in the Ryukyus; there are also substantial Japanese-speaking communities in the United States and Brazil. The Japanese language may be distantly related to Korean, and perhaps also to the Altaic language family, which includes Mongolian and Turkish. For all practical purposes, however, Japanese stands alone, with a grammatical structure unlike that of any other language. One unique feature of Japanese, for example, is the very large role that relative levels of courtesy play in the grammar. *Say It in Japanese* provides many grammatically and socially correct expressions which will be useful to the traveler or foreign resident in Japan. The Japanese text of this book is in Standard Japanese, which is based on the language spoken by educated people from Tokyo, and is that used in the media and the schools. Though there are some dialects of Japanese which are hard for other Japanese speakers to understand, Standard Japanese will be understood wherever Japanese is spoken.

Japanese is ordinarily written in characters (*kanji*) originally borrowed from Chinese, together with phonetic symbols (*kana*) representing syllables rather than single sounds. There are also two standard systems for writing Japanese in Roman letters (*Rōmaji*); this book makes use of the modified Hepburn system, in which consonants are pronounced as in English and vowels as in Italian (see the "Pronunciation" section below for details). The written Japanese characters for each phrase have been included for those who wish to use them for reference and further study. They also provide another means of communication, since they may be pointed out to a speaker of Japanese. Because the Japanese writing in our book follows the entries in Roman letters, it is written from left to right and horizontally, rather than from top to bottom and right to left as in standard Japanese practice.

NOTES ON THE USE OF THIS BOOK

The words, phrases and sentences in this book have been selected to provide for the communication needs of the traveler or foreign resident in Japan, and they have been divided into sections according to the situations likely to be encountered in travel and in daily life. Sections consisting of word lists are in alphabetical order for easy reference. The index at the back of the book enables you to find a specific word or phrase quickly, and also serves as a handy English-Japanese glossary. With the aid of the index or a bilingual dictionary, many sentence patterns given here will answer innumerable needs. For example, the place occupied by "Friday" in the entry

We plan to stay here until [Friday].

may be filled with another word in accordance with your plans. In other sentences, the words in square brackets can be replaced with words immediately following (in the same sentence or in the indented entries below it). Thus the entry

These things to the [left] [right] belong to me.

provides two sentences, "These things to the left belong to me" and "These things to the right belong to me." Three sentences are provided by the following entries:

Give me a seat [on the aisle].
[Tsūrogawa] no seki ni shite kudasai.

—by a window.
Madogiwa—.
—by the emergency exit.
Hijōguchi no soba—.

Note that the substitutions are made at the beginning of the Japanese sentence in this case. Because Japanese grammar is so different from that of Western languages, you would be well advised to stay close to the forms given here in making substitutions. As your Japanese vocabulary grows, you will find you can express an increasingly wide range of thoughts by using the patterns given in this book.

Please note that while brackets always indicate the possibility of substitution, parentheses enclose synonyms or alternative usage for an entry, as in

I am sorry (OR: Pardon me).

Parentheses are also used to explain a word or some nuance of meaning that may be implicit in either the Japanese or English phrase. The abbreviation LIT. is used whenever a more literal translation of a Japanese phrase is provided.

You will notice the word "please" has been omitted from many of the English sentences, in order to save space and avoid repetition. Since "*kudasai*," which is usually used to form polite requests in Japanese, requires a verbal participle as the main verb in the sentence, every Japanese sentence given here is complete as it stands at the proper level of politeness. To be especially polite, you may add "*dōzo*" to the beginning of the sentence. A concise explanation of all the Japanese grammar you need for everyday conversation, E. F. Bleiler's *Essential Japanese Grammar*, is available from Dover Publications, 31 East 2nd Street, Mineola, New York.

You will find the extensive index at the back of the book especially helpful. Capitalized items in the index refer to the section headings and give the number of the page on which the section begins. All other numbers refer to the individual *entries*, which are numbered consecutively throughout the book.

PRONUNCIATION

Japanese is relatively easy for an English-speaker to pronounce, since there are very few sounds that do not appear in English, and Japanese sound combinations are simple. The following table will summarize the most important features:

a   as in f*a*ther
ā   as in f*a*ther, but held longer
b   as in *b*at
ch   as in *ch*at
d   as in *d*ental
e   as in m*e*n
ē   as in m*e*n, but held longer
f   unlike English *f*. Formed by bringing the lower lip up so that it almost touches the upper lip, then holding the position and trying to say an *f*. (English *f*, on the other hand, is formed by bringing the lower lip up to touch the teeth.) If you cannot manage the Japanese *f*, the English *f* will always be intelligible.
g   as in *g*o. In the middle of words and in the particle *ga* in standard Japanese, *g* is often pronounced like *ng* in so*ng*. But an English *g* is always intelligible and correct.
h   as in *h*ome. In the syllable *hi*, however, *h* is pronounced like the *ch* in German '*ich*' (something like an exaggerated pronunciation of the *h* in *h*uge).
i   as in ben*zi*ne.
ii, ī   as in ben*zi*ne, but held longer. *ii* is used in native Japanese words, while *ī* is used in foreign

borrowings. (*ii*, unlike *ī*, is pronounced with the suggestion of two separate vowels.)

j	as in *j*olly
k	as in *k*angaroo
m	as in *m*at
n	as in *n*et. At the end of words *n* is often pronounced by Tokyo speakers as if it were halfway between *n* and *ng* (in si*ng*). An ordinary *n* is always intelligible, and is not incorrect.
o	as in *n*o*t*ify. Pronounce this as a single pure sound, not as a diphthong; English *o* is a diphthong of *o–u*.
ō	as in n*o*tify, but held longer
p	as in *sp*ry. Do not make an *h* sound after the sound *p*, as we do in English in words like *p*in or *p*et.
r	unlike English *r*. Made with a single flip of the tip of the tongue against the ridge behind your upper front teeth. It often sounds like a *d* to an English ear.
s	as in *s*ay
sh	as in *sh*e
t	as in s*t*op. Do not make an *h* sound after the sound *t*, as we do in English in words like *t*in or *t*en.
u	as in f*oo*d. Do not round the corners of your mouth when you make this sound; draw them back.
ū	as in f*oo*d, but held longer
w	as in *w*ash
y	as in *y*ard. *y* is a consonant, not a vowel.
z	as in *z*one

The long vowels *ā*, *ē*, *ii* (or *ī*), *ō*, *ū* are considered different letters from the short vowels, and must be given their full value (approximately twice the length of the short vowels).

An incorrect long or short vowel can change the meaning of a word: *toru* means "to take," while *tōru* means "to pass."

Observe double consonants very closely in Japanese; they are often necessary to distinguish between otherwise identical words. For example, *kite* means "come," and *kitte* means "postage stamp." (Compare the *t* sound in re*t*ail with that in ra*t t*ail.) Note that double *sh* (which is much like the sound in fre*sh sh*eets) is spelled *ssh*.

In some situations the letters *i* and *u* are not fully sounded. This usually occurs between voiceless consonants (*p, ch, ts, s, k, sh*) or after a voiceless consonant at the end of a phrase. In such instances *i* and *u* are whispered or not pronounced at all. A few common examples: *-masu* is pronounced *-mas*, *-mashita* is pronounced *-mashta*, *desu* is pronounced *des* and *watakushi* is pronounced *watakshi*. This aspect of Japanese pronunciation is subject to a great deal of variation and many exceptions; the best way to get an understanding of it is by listening to recorded Japanese speech, such as that found on *Listen & Learn Japanese*, available from Dover Publications on records or cassettes.

Do not stress certain syllables and swallow others; Japanese does not have a strong stress system like English. Instead, pronounce each sound clearly and distinctly, with a moderate, even stress. Pitch of the voice, though it does enter into Japanese, is best ignored by the beginner, since it is difficult to master and only occasionally important.

EVERYDAY PHRASES

1. Hello (OR: **Good day**; OR: **Good afternoon**).
Konnichi wa. 今日は。

2. Good morning. Ohayō gozaimasu.
お早うございます。

3. Good evening. Komban wa. 今晩は。

4. Good night. Oyasumi nasai. おやすみなさい。

5. Welcome. Yōkoso (OR: Irasshaimase).
ようこそ（いらっしゃいませ）。

6. Goodbye. Sayonara (OR: Sayōnara). ✓ あさようなら
さよなら（左様なら）。

7. See you later. Dewa mata. では又。

8. Yes. Hai (OR: Ē). はい（えー）。

9. No. Iie. いゝえ。

10. Perhaps (OR: **Maybe**; OR: **Probably**). Tabun. ☆
多分。

11. Please.* Dōzo. どうぞ。

---

* This word is usually used alone only when offering something.
It may be used at the beginning of polite requests ending in *kudasai*
(roughly meaning "condescend to"), which, however, renders requests
sufficiently polite by itself. In this book, *kudasai* has been included
in all appropriate phrases, though the English entry does not necessarily
include the word "please."

1

12. Excuse me. Shitsurei (OR: Sumimasen).
失礼（済みません）。

13. Thanks [very much].
[Dōmo] arigatō [gozaimasu] (OR: Dōmo).
［どうも］ありがとう［ございます］（どうも）。

14. You are welcome (OR: **Don't mention it**).
Dō itashimashite. どう致しまして。

15. All right (OR: **Very good**). Kekkō desu.
結構です。

16. It doesn't matter. Kamaimasen. 構いません。
かまいません

17. Don't bother.
Dōzo okamai naku (OR: Kamawanaide kudasai).
どうぞお構いなく（構わないで下さい）。

18. I am sorry (OR: **Pardon me**).
Sumimasen (OR: Gomen nasai).
済みません（ごめんなさい）。

19. I am sorry (regret or disappointment). Zannen desu.
残念です。

20. Thank you very much for your kindness.
Goshinsetsu o makoto ni arigatō.
御親切を誠にありがとう。

21. You have been very helpful.
Taihen osewa ni narimashita.
大変お世話になりました。

22. Come in. Dōzo ohairi kudasai.
どうぞお入り下さい。

23. Come here. Koko e kite kudasai.
こゝへ来て下さい。

24. Come along (with me). Issho ni kite kudasai.
一緒に来て下さい。

25. Come back later. Ato de kite kudasai.
後で来て下さい。

26. Come early. Hayame ni kite kudasai.
早目に来て下さい。

27. Wait a minute. Chotto matte kudasai.
ちよつと待つて下さい。

28. Wait for us. Matte kudasai. 待つて下さい。

29. Yet (OR: Not yet). Mada. まだ。

30. Not now. Ima ja naku. 今じやなく。

31. Later. Ato de. 後で。

32. Listen! (OR: Say!) Anonē! あのねー。

33. Look out! Abunai! 危ない!

34. Be careful. Ki o tsukete kudasai.
気を付けて下さい。

35. Take care of yourself. Dōzo odaiji ni.
どうぞお大事に。

SOCIAL PHRASES

36. May I introduce [Mr. (OR: Mrs. OR: Miss) Yamada].
[Yamada San] o goshōkai shimasu.*
［山田さん］を御紹介します。

37. I am glad to meet you.
Dōzo yoroshiku (OR: Hajimemashite).
どうぞ宜しく（初めまして）。

38. How are you? (OR: How do you do?)
Ikaga desu ka? (OR: Genki desu ka?) いかが
如何ですか？（元気ですか？）

39. Very well. And you?   Okagesama de. Sochira wa?
お陰様で。そちらは？

40. Very well, thanks.   Okagesama de genki desu.
お陰様で元気です。

41. How are things?   Dō desu ka? どうですか？

42. So, so.   Mā, mā. まあまあ。

43. Please sit down.
Okake kudasai (OR: Dōzo osuwari kudasai).
お掛け下さい（どうぞお座り下さい）。

44. It's a pleasure to see you again.
Mata ome ni kakarete ureshii desu.
又お目にかかれて嬉しいです。

45. Congratulations.   Omedetō gozaimasu.
おめでとうございます。

* In Japanese, *San* is added after the surname for all forms of address.

46. Happy birthday. Otanjōbi omedetō.
お誕生日おめびとう。

47. I like you very much. Hontō ni suki desu.
本当に好きです。

48. I love you. Daisuki desu. 大好きです。

49. May I see you again? Mata <u>aimashō</u> ka?
又会いましようか？

あいましょう
会

50. Let's meet again next week. Raishū mata aimashō.
来週又会いましよう。

51. I have enjoyed myself very much.
Taihen tanoshikatta desu. 大変楽しかつたです。

52. Give my regards to [your friend].
[Anata no otomodachi] ni yoroshiku.
[あなたのお友達]に宜しく。

BASIC QUESTIONS

53. What? Nan desu ka? 何ですか？

54. Pardon? (OR: **What did you say?**) Shitsurei?
失礼？

55. What is [this] [that]? [Kore] [Sore] wa nan desu ka?
[これ][それ]は何ですか？

56. What happened? Dō shimashita? どうしました？

57. What is the matter? (OR: **Is anything wrong?**)
Dōka shimashita ka? どうかしましたか？

58. What do you want? Nan no goyō desu ka?
何の御用ですか？

59. When? Itsu? いつ？

60. When does it [leave]? Itsu [demasu] ka?
いつ[出ます]か？

61. —arrive. —tsukimasu. 一着きます。

62. —begin. —hajimarimasu. 一始まります。

63. —end. —owarimasu. 一終ります。

64. Where? Doko desu ka? どこですか？

65. Where to? Dochira e? どちらへ？

66. Where is [it]? [Sore wa] doko desu ka?
[それは] どこですか？

67. Why? Naze desu ka? なぜですか？

68. How? Dō desu ka? どうですか？

69. How long (time)? Dono kurai nagaku?
どの位長く？

70. How far? (OR: **How near?**)
Kyori wa dono kurai desu ka?
距離はどの位ですか？

71. How much? Dono kurai desu ka?
どの位ですか？
も くらい

72. How much (in price)? Ikura desu ka?
いくらですか?

73. How many? Ikutsu desu ka?
いくつですか?

74. How do you do it? (OR: How does it work?)
Dō suru no desu ka? どうするのですか?

75. Who? Dare? (OR: Donata?)
誰? (どなた?)

76. Who are you? Donata desu ka?
どなたですか?

77. Who is [that boy]?
[Ano otoko no ko] wa dare desu ka?
[あの男の子] は誰ですか?

78. —that girl. Ano onna no ko—.
あの女の子 一。

79. —that man. Ano otoko no hito—.
あの男の人一。

80. —this woman. Kono onna no hito—.
この女の人 一。

81. Am I on time? Jikan dōri desu ka?
時間通りですか?

82. Am I early? Haya sugimashita ka?
早過ぎましたか?

83. Am I late? Okuremashita ka?
遅れましたか?

TALKING ABOUT YOURSELF

84. What is your name? Onamae wa? お名前は?

85. I am [Mr. Sugiyama].
Watakushi wa [Sugiyama] desu.
私は[杉山]です。

86. My name is [John].
Watakushi no namae wa [Jon] desu.
私の名前は[ジョン]です。

87. I am [21 years old] [an American citizen].
Watakushi wa [nijūissai] [Amerika no shimin] desu.
私は[二十一才][アメリカの市民]です。

88. My address is [1–10 Naka Meguro, Meguro-ku, Tokyo].
Watakushi no jūsho wa [Tōkyō-to, Meguro-ku, Naka
Meguro ichi no jū banchi] desu.

私の住所は[東京都目黒区中目黒一の十番地]
です。
　　　　　To
　　　　　ku

89. I am [a student]. Watakushi wa [gakusei] desu.
私は[学生]です。

90. —a teacher. —sensei. 一先生。

91. —a businessman. —kaisha-in (OR: jitsugyōka).
一会社員 (実業家)。

92. What is your job? Anata no shigoto wa nan desu ka?
あなたのお仕事は何ですか?

93. I am a friend of [Mr. Suzuki].
Watakushi wa [Suzuki San] no yūjin desu.　Yūjin
私は[鈴木さん]の友人です。
　　　　　　　　　　　　　　　　　ゆう じん

94. [He] [She] works for [Sony].
[Kare] [Kanojo] wa [Sonii] de hataraite imasu.
[彼] [彼女] は [ソニー] で 働いて います。

95. I am here on [vacation] [business].
Koko e [kyūka] [shōyō] de kimashita.
ここへ [休暇] [商用] で 来ました。

きゅうか
休暇

96. I have been here [one week]. Sudeni [isshūkan] imasu.
既に [一週間] います。

いっしゅう 一週

97. We plan to stay here until [Friday].
[Kin-yōbi] made iru tsumori desu.
[金曜日] までいる積りです。

98. I am going to [Kyoto]. [Kyōto] e ikimasu.
[京都] へ行きます。

99. I am in a hurry. Isoide imasu. 急いでいます。

100. I am [cold] [hot]. [Samui] [Atsui] desu.
[寒い] [暑い] です。

101. I am hungry. Onaka ga sukimashita.
お腹がすきました。

102. I am thirsty. Nodo ga kawakimashita.
喉が乾きました。

103. I am busy. Watakushi wa isogashii desu.
私は忙しいです。

104. I have a previous engagement. Sen-yaku ga arimasu.
先約が有ります。

105. I am tired. Tsukaremashita. 疲れました。

106. [We are] [I am] [He is] [She is] [You are]
   [They are] happy.*
Ureshii [desu].   嬉しい[です]。

107. I am [glad].   [Yorokonde] imasu.
[喜んで]います。

108. I am [angry].   [Okotte] imasu. [怒って]います。

109. I am [sad].   [Kanashii] desu. [悲しい]です。

110. —depressed.   Yūutsu—. 憂うつ—。

111. —lonely.   Sabishii—. 寂しい—。

112. I am disappointed.   Gakkari shimashita.
がっかりしました。

113. I cannot do it.   Sore wa dekimasen.
それは出来ません。—

MAKING YOURSELF
UNDERSTOOD

114. Do you speak [English]?   [Eigo] ga dekimasu ka?
[英語]が出来ますか?

115. Does anyone here speak [French]?
[Furansugo] no dekiru mono wa imasen ka?
[フランス語]の出来る者はいませんか?

---

* Japanese verbs do not have different forms to indicate the number or person or gender of the subject of the sentence. The same forms are used whether the subject is I or you or they or anything else. Thus the verb form *kaimasu* could mean I buy, you (SING.) buy, he buys, she buys, it buys, we buy, you (PL.) buy, or they buy.

116. I speak a little [German].
[Doitsugo] ga sukoshi dekimasu.
［ドイツ語］が少し出来ます。

すこ
少し

117. [Speak] more slowly.
Motto yukkuri [itte (OR: hanashite)] kudasai.
もつとゆつくり［言つて（話して）］下さい。

はなして

118. I understand.   Wakarimashita. 分りました。

119. I do not understand.   Wakarimasen. 分りません。

120. Do you understand?   Wakarimasu ka?
分りますか？

121. I know.   Shitte imasu. 知つています。

し
知る(工)

122. I do not know.   Shirimasen. 知りません。

123. I think so.   Sō da to omoimasu.
そうだと思います。

124. Repeat it.   Kurikaeshite kudasai.
繰り返して下さい。

125. Write it down.   Kaite kudasai. 書いて下さい。

126. That is right.   Sore wa tadashii no desu.
それは正しいのです。

127. That is wrong.   Sore wa machigai desu.
それは間違いです。

128. What does [this character (OR: symbol)] mean?
[Kono kanji] wa nan desu ka?
［この漢字］は何ですか？

129. What does this word mean? (LIT: **What is the meaning of this word?**)
Kono kotoba no imi wa? この言葉の意味は?

130. How do you say ["pencil"] in Japanese?
Nihongo de ["pencil"] wa dō iimasu ka?

日本語で[pencil]はどう言いますか?

131. Please write it in Roman letters.
Rōmaji de kaite kudasai.

ローマ字で書いて下さい。

DIFFICULTIES AND MISUNDERSTANDINGS

132. Where is [the American embassy]?
[Amerika taishikan] wa doko desu ka?

[アメリカ大使館]はどこですか?

133. —the consulate. Ryōjikan—. 領事館—。

134. —the police station. Keisatsu—. 警察—。

135. —the lost-and-found office. Ishitsubutsugakari—.
遺失物係—。

136. I want to see [the manager].
[Shihainin] ni aitai no desu ga.
[支配人]に会いたいのですが。

137. —the person in charge. Kakari no mono—.
係の者—。

138. Can you help me? Onegai dekimasu ka?
お願い出来ますか?

139. Please help me.   Chotto onegai shimasu.

ちょっとお願いします。

140. I am looking for my friend.

Tomodachi o sagashite iru no desu ga.

友達を捜しているのですが。

さが
捜して

141. I have lost my way.   Mayotte shimaimashita.

迷ってしまいました。

142. I cannot find [the address].

[Jūsho] ga mitsukarimasen.   [住所]が見付かりません。

143. She has lost [her handbag].

[Handobaggu] o nakushimashita.

[ハンドバッグ]を無くしました。

144. I have lost my passport.

[Pasupōto] o nakushimashita.

[パスポート]をなくしました。

わす
忘れました

145. We forgot our [keys].   [Kagi] o wasuremashita.

[鍵]を忘れました。

146. We missed [the train].   [Kisha] ni noriokuremashita.

[汽車]に乗り遅れました。

147. It is not my fault.   Watakushi no sei dewa arimasen.

私のせいではありません。

148. I do not remember [the name].

[Namae] wa oboete imasen. [名前]は覚えていません。

149. What shall I do?   Dō shimashō ka?

どうしましょうか?

150. Leave us alone. Kamawanai de kudasai.

構わないで下さい。

151. Help! Tasukete! 助けて！

152. Thief! Dorobō! 泥棒！ どろぼう

153. Fire! Kaji! 火事！

154. This is an emergency. Hijōji desu.

非常時です。

CUSTOMS

155. Where is [the customs office]?
[Zeikan] wa doko deshō ka?

[税関]はどこでしようか？

156. Here is my [baggage].
Kore ga watakushi no [nimotsu] desu.

これが私の[荷物]です。

157. —passport. —pasupōto (OR: ryoken).

ーパスポート（旅券）。

158. —identification card. —mibun shōmeisho.

ー身分証明書。

159. —health certificate. —kenkō shōmeisho.

ー健康証明書。

160. —visa. —biza. ービザ。

161. I am in transit. Ichiji nyūkoku desu.

ー時入国です。

162. [The baggage] over there is mine.
Ano [nimotsu] ga watakushi no desu.
あの [荷物] が私のです。

163. Must I open everything?   Zembu akeru no desu ka?
全部 開けるのですか？

164. I cannot open this [trunk].
Kono [toranku] wa akeraremasen.
この [トランク] は開けられません。

165. There is [nothing but clothing] here.
Kore wa [ifuku dake] desu. これは [衣服だけ] です。

166. I have nothing to declare.
Shinkokusuru mono wa arimasen.
申告する物はありません。

167. Everything is for my personal use.
Mina watakushi no temawarihin desu.
皆私の手回り品です。

168. I bought this [necklace] in the United States.
Kono [nekkurēsu] wa Amerika de kaimashita.
この [ネックレース] はアメリカで買いました。

169. These are [gifts].   Kore wa [miyagemono] desu.
これは [土産物] です。

170. This is all there is.   Kore de zembu desu.
これで全部です。

171. Must duty be paid on [these things]?
[Kore] ni wa kanzei ga kakarimasu ka?
[これ] には関税がかかりますか？

172. Have you finished yet? Mō sumimashita ka?

もう済みましたか？

BAGGAGE

173. Where can we check our luggage through to [Nagasaki]?
[Nagasaki] ekidome no nimotsu no kakari wa doko desu ka?

［長崎］駅止めの荷物の係はどこびすか？

174. These things to the [left] [right] belong to me.
Kono [hidarite] [migite] no mono wa watakushi no desu.

この［左手］［右手］の物は私のびす。

175. I cannot find all my baggage.
Mada miataranai nimotsu ga arimasu.

まだ見当らない荷物があります。

176. One [package] is missing.
Hitotsu [kozutsumi] ga arimasen.

一つ［小包］がありません。

177. I want to leave this [suitcase] here for [a few days].
Kono [sūtsukēsu] o [nisannichi] azuketai no desu ga.

この［スーツケース］を［二、三日］預けたいのびすが。

178. Give me a receipt for the baggage.
Nimotsu no azukarishō o kudasai.

荷物の預かり証を下さい。

179. I have [a black bag]. [Kuroi kaban] o motte imasu.

［黒い鞄］を持っています。

180. I have [four] pieces of luggage altogether.
Nimotsu wa zembu de [yonko] desu.
荷物は全部で［四箇］です。

181. Carry these to the baggage room.
Kore o tenimotsu toriatsukaijo e hakonde kudasai.
これを手荷物取り扱い所へ運んで下さい。

182. Don't forget that.   Are o wasurenaide kudasai.
あれを忘れないで下さい。

183. I shall carry this myself.
Kore wa jibun de motte ikimasu.
これは自分で持って行きます。

184. Follow me.   Tsuitekite kudasai. 付いて来て下さい。

185. Get me [a taxi] [a porter].
[Takushī] [Akabō] o yonde kudasai.
［タクシー］［赤帽］を呼んで下さい。

186. This is very fragile.   Kore wa kowaremono desu.
これは壊れ物です。

187. Handle this carefully.   Toriatsukai ni chūi negaimasu.
取り扱いに注意願います。

188. How much do I owe you? (LIT: How much is it?)
Ikura desu ka?   いくうですか？

189. Should I leave a tip?*   Chippu wa irimasu ka?
チップは要りますか？

* Tipping is not widely prevalent in Japan.

TRAVEL DIRECTIONS

190. I want to go to [the airline office].
[Kōkūgaisha] ni ikitai no desu ga.
［航空会社］に行きたいのですが。

191. —the travel agent's office. Ryokō annaijo—.
旅行案内所 一。

192. —the Japan Travel Bureau. Nihon Kōtsū Kōsha—.
日本交通公社 一。

193. How long does it take to walk to [the Ginza]?
[Ginza] made aruite donokurai desu ka?
［銀座］まで歩いてどの位ですか？

194. Is this the shortest way to [Akasaka]?
[Akasaka] e no chikamichi desu ka?
［赤坂］への近道ですか？

195. Show me the way to [the center of town].
[Chūō chiku] ni iku michijun o oshiete kudasai.
［中央地区］に行く道順を教えて下さい。

196. —the shopping section. Hankagai—. 繁華街 一。

197. —downtown. Shitamachi—. 下町 一。

198. —the residential section. Jūtaku chiku—.
住宅地区 一。

199. Do I turn to [the north]?
[Kita] no hō e magaru no desu ka? ［北］の方へ曲がるのですか

200. —the south. Minami—. 南 一。

201. —the east.　Higashi—.　東一.

202. —the west.　Nishi—.　西一.

203. —the right.　Migi—.　右一.

204. —the left.　Hidari—.　左一.

205. What street is this?　Kore wa nan to yū tōri desu ka?
これは何と言う通りですか?

206. How far is it?　Dono kurai tōi deshō ka?
どの位遠いでしようか?

207. Is it [near] [far]?　[Chikai] [tōi] deshō ka?
[近い][遠い]でしようか?

208. Can we walk there?　Aruite ikemasu ka?
歩いて行けますか?

209. Am I going in the right direction?
Kono hōkō de ii no deshō ka?
この方向でいゝのでしようか?

210. Please point.　Yubi sashite kudasai.
指差して下さい.

211. Is it [this way]?　[Kochira no hōkō] desu ka?
[こちらの方向]ですか?

212. —that way.　Achira no hōkō—.　あちらの方向一.

213. Turn [left] [right] at the next corner.
Tsugi no kado de [hidari] [migi] e magaru no desu.
次の角で[左][右]へ曲がるのです.

214. Is it on [this side] of the street?
Michi no [kochiragawa] desu ka?
道の[こちら側]ですか?

215. —the other side. —achiragawa. —あちら側.

216. Is it [across the bridge]? [Hashi no mukō] desu ka?
[橋の向こう]ですか?

217. —under the elevated tracks. Gādo no shita—.
ガードの下—.

218. —beyond the traffic light. Kōtsū shingō no saki—.
交通信号の先—.

219. —next to the apartment house. Apāto no tonari—.
アパートの隣り—.

220. —in the middle of this side of the block.
Kochiragawa no mannaka hen—.
こちら側の真中辺—.

221. —straight ahead. Massugu saki—. 真つ直ぐ先—.

222. —toward the back. Ushiro no hō—.
後の方—.

223. —inside the station. Eki no naka—.
駅の中—.

224. —near the square. Hiroba no soba—.
広場の側—.

225. —near the hotel. Hoteru no chikaku—.
ホテルの近く—.

226. —outside the lobby. Robī no soto—. ロビーの外ー.

227. —at the entrance. Iriguchi no tokoro—.
入口の所ー.

228. —opposite the park. Kōen no mukai—.
公園の向かいー.

229. —beside the school. Gakkō no waki—.
学校の脇ー.

230. —in front of the statue. Dōzō no mae—.
銅像の前ー.

231. —in the rear of the store. Mise no oku—.
店の奥ー.

232. —behind the building. Biru no ura—.
ビルの裏ー.

233. —up the hill. Saka no ue—. 坂の上ー.

234. —down the stairs. Kaidan no shita—.
階段の下ー.

235. —at the top of the escalator. Esukarētā no ue—.
エスカレーターの上ー.

236. —over the exit. Deguchi no ue—.
出口の上ー.

237. A luxury apartment house. Manshon. マンション.

238. The factory. Kōjō (OR: Kōba). 工場.

239. The office building. Biru. ビル.

240. The suburbs. Kōgai. 郊外.

241. The city (OR: town). Machi. 町.

242. The country (nation). Kuni. 国.

243. The country (countryside). Inaka. 田舎.

244. The village. Mura. 村.

BOAT

245. When must I go on board? Jōsen wa itsu desu ka?
乗船 は いつ です か?

246. Bon voyage! Gobuji de itte irasshai!
御無事 で 行つ て いらつ しやい!

247. I want to rent a deck chair.
Dekki chea o karitai no desu ga.
デッキ・チェア を 借りたい の で す が.

248. Can we go ashore at [Kobe]?
[Kōbe] de jōriku dekimasu ka?
[神戸] で 上陸 出来ます か?

249. At what time is dinner served?
Yūshoku wa nanji desu ka? 夕食 は 何 時です か?

250. When is the [first sitting] [second sitting]?
[Ikkaime] [nikaime] no wa itsu desu ka?
[一回目][二回目] の は いつ です か?

251. I feel seasick. Fune ni yoimashita.
船 に 酔い ました.

252. Have you a remedy for seasickness?
Yoidome wa arimasen ka? 酔い止めはありませんか?

253. Lifeboat. Kyūmeitei. 救命艇。

254. Life preserver. Kyūmeibukuro. 救命袋。

255. The ferry. Watashi. 渡し。

256. The dock. Hatoba. 波止場。

257. The cabin. Senshitsu. 船室。

258. The deck. Dekki. デッキ。

259. The pool. Pūru. プール。

260. The captain. Senchō. 船長。

261. The purser. Jimuchō. 事務長。

262. The cabin steward. Bōi-san. ボーイさん。

263. The dining room steward. Wētā. ウェーター。

AIRPLANE

264. I want to make a reservation.
Yoyaku shitai no desu ga. 予約したいのですが。

265. I want to cancel a reservation.
Yoyaku o torikeshitai no desu ga.
予約を取消したいのですが。

266. When is the next flight to [Osaka]?
[Ōsaka]-yuki no tsugi no bin wa itsu desu ka?
[大阪]行の次の便はいつですか？

267. When does the plane arrive at [Narita]?
Hikōki wa [Narita] e itsu tsukimasu ka?
飛行機は[成田]へいつ着きますか？

268. What kind of plane is used on that flight?
Sono bin wa donna hikōki desu ka?
その便はどんな飛行機ですか？

269. Will food be served?   Shokuji wa demasu ka?
食事は出ますか？

270. May I confirm the reservation by telephone?
Yoyaku no kakunin wa denwa de dekimasu ka?
予約の確認は電話で出来ますか？

271. At what time should we check in at [the airport]?
[Kūkō] e nanji ni ikeba ii deshō ka?
[空港]へ何時に行けばいゝでしょうか？

272. How long does it take to get to the airport from my hotel?
Hoteru kara kūkō made nampun-gurai desu ka?
ホテルから空港まで何分位ですか？

273. Is there bus service between the airport and the city?
Kūkō kara shinai made basu no sābisu ga arimasu ka?
空港から市内まで バスのサービスがありますか？

274. Is that flight nonstop?
Sono bin wa chokkō desu ka?
その便は直行ですか？

275. Where does the plane stop en route?
Tochū doko de orimasu ka?
途中どこで下りますか？

276. How long do we stop?   Dono kurai tomarimasu ka?
どの位止まりますか？

277. May I stop over in [Moji]?
Tochū [Moji] de oriraremasu ka?
途中［門司］で降りられますか？

278. We want to travel [first class].
[Ittō-seki] ga ii no desu ga. ［一等席］がいゝのですが。

279. —economy class.   Ekonomi kurasu—.
エコノミ・クラスー。

280. Is flight [22] on time?
[Nijūni]-bin wa jikan dōri desu ka?
［二十二］便は時間通りですか？

281. What is the baggage allowance?
Nimotsu no jūryō seigen wa?
荷物の重量制限は？

282. How much per kilo for excess?
Chōkaryō wa ichi kiro ikura desu ka?
超過料は一キロいくらですか？

283. May I carry this on board?
Kore wa mochikomemasu ka?
これは持ち込めますか？

284. Give me a seat [on the aisle].
[Tsūrogawa] no seki ni shite kudasai.
［通路側］の席にして下さい。

285. —by a window. Madogiwa—. 窓際 —。

286. —by the emergency exit. Hijōguchi no soba—.
非常口の側 —。

287. May we board the plane now?
Hikōki ni norikonde ii desu ka?
飛行機に乗り込んでいいですか？

288. From which gate does my flight leave?
Kono bin wa dono gēto desu ka?
この便はどのゲートですか？

289. Call the stewardess. Suchuwadesu o yonde kudasai.
スチュワデスを呼んで下さい。

290. Fasten your seat belt.
Shīto beruto o shimete kudasai.
シート・ベルトを締めて下さい。

291. May I smoke? Tabako o sutte mo kamaimasen ka?
タバコを吸っても構いませんか？

292. Will we arrive [on time]?
[Yotei dōri ni] tsukimasu ka?
[予定通りに] 着きますか？

293. —late. Yotei yori okurete—. 予定より遅れて —。

294. This is an announcement. Gohōkoku itashimasu.
御報告致します。

295. A boarding pass. Norikomi ken. 乗り込み券。

296. The limousine. Rimojin. リモジン。

TRAIN

297. When does the ticket office [open] [close]?
Shussatsuguchi wa itsu [akimasu] [shimarimasu] ka?
出札口はいつ[開きます][締まります]か?

298. When is the next train for [Hiroshima]?
Tsugi no [Hiroshima]-yuki wa itsu demasu ka?
次の[広島]行きはいつ出ますか?

299. Is there [an earlier] [a later] train?
Sore yori [hayaku] [osoku] deru no wa arimasen ka?
それより[早く][遅く]出るのはありませんか?

300. Is there [an express] [a local] train?
[Kyūkō] [Futsū] ressha wa arimasen ka?
[急行][普通]列車はありませんか?

301. From which platform does the train leave?
Dono hōmu kara demasu ka?
どのホームから出ますか?

302. Where can I get a timetable?
Jikokuhyō wa doko de moraemasu ka?
時刻表はどこでもらえますか?

303. Does this train stop at [Nara]?
Kono kisha wa [Nara] de tomarimasu ka?
この汽車は[奈良]で止まりますか?

304. Is there time to get off?
Oriru jikan wa arimasu ka? 降りる時間はありますか?

305. When do we arrive?   Itsu tsukimasu ka?
いつ着きますか?

306. Is this seat free? Kono seki wa aite imasu ka?
この席は明いていますか？

307. Am I disturbing you? Ojama desu ka?
お邪魔ですか？

308. Open the [window]. [Mado] o akete kudasai.
[窓] をあけて下さい。

309. Close the [door]. [Doa] o shimete kudasai.
[ドア] を締めて下さい。

310. Where are we now? Koko wa doko desu ka?
こゝはどこですか？

311. Is the train on time? Kisha wa jikan dōri desu ka?
汽車は時間通りですか？

312. How late are we? Dono kurai okuremashita ka?
どの位遅れましたか？

313. The conductor. Shashō. 車掌。

314. The ticket gate. Kaisatsuguchi. 改札口。

315. The information office. Uketsuke. 受付け。

316. A one-way ticket. Katamichi jōshaken.
片道乗車券。

317. A round-trip ticket. Ōfukuken. 往復券。

318. A platform ticket. Nyūjōken. 入場券。

319. The railroad station. Sutēshon (OR: Eki).
ステーション（駅）。

320. The waiting room. Machiaishitsu. 待合室。

321. The sleeping car. Shindaisha. 寝台車。

322. The dining car. Shokudōsha. 食堂車。

BUS, SUBWAY AND STREETCAR

323. Where does [the streetcar] stop?
[Densha] wa doko de tomarimasu ka?
[電車] はどこで止まりますか?

324. Where is the nearest [subway station]?
Ichiban chikai [chikatetsu] wa doko desu ka?
一番近い [地下鉄] はどこですか?

325. How often does [the bus] run?
[Basu] wa nampun-oki desu ka?
[バス] は何分置きですか?

326. Which bus goes to [Shibuya]?
Dono basu ga [Shibuya] e ikimasu ka?
どのバスが [渋谷] へ行きますか?

327. How much is the fare? Jōsharyō wa ikura desu ka?
乗車料はいくらですか?

328. Do you go by [the Imperial Palace]?
[Kyūjō] no soba o tōrimasu ka?
[宮城] の側を通りますか?

329. I want to get off [at the next stop] [right here].
[Tsugi no teiryūjo de] [Koko de] oritai no desu.
[次の停留所で][ここで] 降りたいのです。

330. Please tell me where to get off.
Oriru tokoro o oshiete kudasai.
降りる所を教えて下さい。

331. Will I have to change?   Norikae wa arimasu ka?
乗り換えはありますか？

332. Where do we transfer?   Doko de norikae desu ka?
どこで乗り換えですか？

333. The driver.   Untenshu.   運転手。

334. The transfer.   Norikaeken.   乗り換え券。

335. The bus stop.   Basu no teiryūjo. バスの停留所。

TAXI

336. Call a taxi for me.   Takushī o yonde kudasai.
タクシーを呼んで下さい。

337. Are you free, (driver)?   Aite imasu ka?
空いていますか？

338. What do you charge [per hour]?
[Ichi jikan] ikura desu ka? [一時間] いくらですか？

339. —per kilometer.   Ichi kiro—.   一キロ一。

340. —per day.   Ichi nichi—.   一日一。

341. Take me to this address.   Kono jūsho e itte kudasai.
この住所へ行って下さい。

342. How much will the ride cost?
Soko made ikura desu ka? そこまで いくらですか？

343. How long will it take to get there?
Soko made dono kurai kakarimasu ka?
そこまで どの位 掛かりますか？

344. Drive us around [for one hour].
[Ichi jikan gurai] norimawashite kudasai.
[一時間位] 乗り回わして下さい。

345. Drive more carefully.
Motto chūi shite unten negaimasu.
もっと注意して運転願います。

346. Drive more slowly.   Motto yukkuri hashitte kudasai.
もっとゆっくり走って下さい。

347. I am not in a great hurry.   Betsu ni isoide wa imasen.
別に急いではいません。

348. Stop [here].   [Koko de] tomete kudasai.
[こゝで] 止めて下さい。

349. Wait for me here.   Matte ite kudasai.
待っていて下さい。

350. I will return in [five minutes].
[Gofun] de modotte kimasu.
[五分] で戻って来ます。

351. Keep the change.   Otsuri wa totte oite kudasai.
おつりは取って置いて下さい。

352. The taxi stand.   Takushī noriba. タクシー乗り場。

353. The taxi meter. Takushī no mētā. タクシーのメーター。

RENTING AUTOS AND OTHER VEHICLES

354. What kind of [cars] do you have?
Donna [kuruma] ga arimasu ka?
どんな [車] がありますか？

355. I have an international driver's license.
Kokusai menkyoshō o motte imasu.
国際免許証を持っています。

356. What is the rate [per day]?
[Ichi nichi] ikura desu ka? [一日] いくらですか？

357. How much additional [per kilometer]?
Sore ijō wa [ichi kiro] ikura desu ka?
それ以上は [一キロ] いくらですか？

358. Are gas and oil also included?
Gasorin to oiru mo fukunde desu ka?
ガソリンと オイルも 含んで ですか？

359. Does the insurance policy cover [personal liability]?
Hoken ni wa [jinshin baishō] mo haitte imasu ka?
保険には [人身賠償] も入っていますか？

360. —property damage. —taibutsu baishō.
一対物賠償。

361. —collision. —shōtotsu baishō. 一衝突賠償。

362. Are the papers in order?
Shorui wa totonotte imasu ka?
書類は整っていますか？

363. I am not familiar with this car.
Kono kuruma wa tsukainarete imasen.
この車は使い慣れていません。

364. Explain [this dial].
Kono [daiaru] wa nanno tame desu ka?
この [ダイアル] は何の為ですか?

365. —this switch. —suitchi. ースイッチ。

366. Show me how [the heater] operates.
[Hītā] no tsukaikata o misete kudasai.
[ヒーター] の使い方を見せて下さい。

367. Will someone pick it up at the hotel?
Hoteru e tori ni kite moraemasu ka?
ホテルへ取りに来てもらえますか?

368. Is the office open all night?
Ofisu wa yodōshi aite imasu ka?
オフィスは夜通し開いていますか?

369. The bicycle. Jitensha. 自転車。

370. The motorcycle. Ōtobai. オートバイ。

371. The motor scooter. Sukūtā. スクーター。

AUTO: DIRECTIONS

372. What is the name of [this city]?
[Kono machi] wa nanto iimasu ka?
[この町] は何と いいますか?

373. How far [to the next town]?
[Tsugi no machi made] dono kurai desu ka?
[次の町まで] どの位ですか?

374. Where does [this road] lead?
[Kono michi] wa doko e ikimasu ka?
[この道] はどこへ行きますか?

375. Are there road signs?
Dōro hyōshiki wa arimasu ka?
道路標識はありますか?

376. Is the road [paved] [rough]?
[Hosō shita] [Areta] dōro desu ka?
[舗装した] [荒れた] 道路ですか?

377. Show me the easiest way.
Kantan na michijun o oshiete kudasai.
簡単な道順を教えて下さい。

378. Show it to me on this [road map].
Kono [zumen] de misete kudasai.
この [図面] で見せて下さい。

379. Can I avoid heavy traffic?
Konzatsu o sakeru koto ga dekimasu ka?
混雑を避けることが出来ますか?

380. May I park here [for a while] [overnight]?
[Shibaraku] [Hitoban] koko e chūsha dekimasu ka?
[暫く] [一晩] ここへ駐車出来ますか?

381. The expressway.   Kōsoku dōro. 高速道路。

382. The fork.   Wakaremichi. 別れ道。

383. The intersection. Kōsaten. 交叉点。

384. The major road. Shuyō dōro. 主要道路。

385. The garage. Garēji. ガレージ。

386. The auto repair shop. Jidōsha shūrijo.
自動車修理所。

387. The parking lot. Chūshajō. 駐車場。

388. The stop sign. Sutoppu no hyōshiki.
ストップの標識。

AUTO: HELP ON THE ROAD

389. My car has broken down.
Kuruma ga koshō shimashita.
車が故障しました。

390. Call a mechanic. Shūrikō o yonde kudasai.
修理工を呼んで下さい。

391. Help me push [the car] to the side.
[Kuruma] o osu no ni te o kashite kudasai.
[車]を押すのに手を貸して下さい。

392. Push me. Oshite kudasai. 押して下さい。

393. Please lend me [a jack].
[Jyakkī] o kashite kudasai. [ジャッキー]を貸して下さい。

394. Change the tire. Taiya o kaete kudasai.
タイヤを換えて下さい。

395. My car is stuck in [the mud] [the ditch].
[Nukarumi] [Mizo] ni hamatte shimaimashita.
[ぬかるみ] [溝] にはまってしまいました。

396. Drive me to the nearest [gas station].
Ichiban chikai [gasorin sutando] e onegai shimasu.
一番近い [ガソリン・スタンド] へお願いします。

AUTO: GAS STATION AND REPAIR SHOP

397. Give me [twenty] liters of [regular] [premium] gasoline.
[Futsū] [Jōkyū] no gasorin o [nijū] rittoru kudasai.
[普通] [上級] のガソリンを [二十] リットル下さい。

398. Fill it up.   Ippai ni shite kudasai.
一杯にして下さい。

399. Change the oil.   Oiru o kaete kudasai.
オイルを替えて下さい。

400. Lubricate the car.   Gurisu appu o negaimasu.
グリス・アップを願います。

401. Put water in the radiator.
Rajiētā ni mizu o irete kudasai.
ラジエーターに水を入れて下さい。

402. Charge the battery.   Denchi no jūden o negaimasu.
電池の充電を願います。

403. Clean the windshield.
Furonto uindō o fuite kudasai.
フロント・ウィンドーを拭いて下さい。

404. Adjust the [brakes].
[Burēki] no chōsetsu o negaimasu.
［ブレーキ］の調節を願います。

405. Check the tire pressure.
Taiya no puresshā o hakatte mite kudasai.
タイヤ のプレッシヤーを計って見て下さい。

406. Repair the [flat tire].   [Panku] o naoshite kudasai.
［パンク］を直して下さい。

407. Could you wash it [now]?
[Ima] aratte moraemasu ka? ［今］洗ってもらえますか？

408. How long must we wait?
Dono kurai matsu no desu ka?
どの位待つのびすか？

409. The motor overheats.   Mōtā ga ōbā hīto shimasu.
モーター がオーバー・ヒートします。

410. Is there a leak?   Morete imasu ka?
洩れていますか？

411. It makes a noise.   Oto o tatemasu.
音を立てます。

412. The lights do not work.   Akari ga tsukimasen.
明りがつきません。

413. The car does not start.   Enjin ga kakarimasen.
エンジンがかゝりません。

PARTS OF THE CAR AND AUTO EQUIPMENT

414. Accelerator.   Akuseru. アクセル。

415. Air filter. Firutā. フィルター。

416. Alcohol. Arukōru. アルコール。

417. Antifreeze. Futō eki. 不凍液。

418. Axle. Shajiku. 車軸。

419. Battery. Batterī. バッテリー。

420. Bolt. Boruto. ボルト。

421. Brakes. Burēki. ブレーキ。

422. Emergency brake. Hijō burēki. 非常ブレーキ。

423. Bumper. Bampā. バンパー。

424. Carburetor. Kyaburētā (OR: Kyabu).
キャブレーター (キャブ)。

425. Chassis. Shadai. 車台。

426. Choke (automatic). Chōku (jidō). チョーク(自動)。

427. Clutch. Kuratchi. クラッチ。

428. Cylinder. Shirindā. シリンダー。

429. Differential. Sadō. 差動。

430. Directional signal. Hōkō shijiki. 方向指示器。

431. Door. Doa (OR: Tobira). ドア(扉)。

432. Electrical system. Denki sōchi. 電気装置。

433. Engine. Enjin. エンジン。

434. Exhaust pipe. Haiki kan. 排気管。

435. Exterior. Gaibu. 外部。

436. Fan. Fan. ファン。

437. Fan belt. Fan beruto. ファン・ベルト。

438. Fender. Fendā. フェンダー。

439. Fire extinguisher. Shōkaki. 消火器。

440. Flashlight. Kaichū dentō. 懐中電燈。

441. Fuel pump. Gasorin pompu. ガソリン・ポンプ。

442. Fuse. Hyūzu. ヒューズ。

443. Gear shift (OR: Manual transmission). Giya shifuto. ギヤ・シフト。

444. First gear. Fāsuto. ファースト。

445. Second gear. Sekando. セカンド。

446. Third gear. Sādo. サード。

447. Fourth gear. Kōsoku giya. 高速ギヤ。

448. Reverse gear. Gyakkō. 逆行。

449. Neutral gear. Nūtoraru. ヌートラル。

450. Grease. Gurīsu. グリース。

451. Generator. Hatsudenki. 発電機。

452. Hammer. Hammā (OR: Kanazuchi). ハンマー（金槌）.

453. Heater. Hītā. ヒーター。

454. Hood. Fuddō. フット゚。

455. Horn. Hōn. ホーン。

456. Horsepower. Bariki. 馬力。

457. Ignition key. Igunisshon. イグニッション。

458. Inner tube. Chūbu. チューブ゚。

459. Instrument panel. Dasshu. ダッシュ。

460. Jack. Jyakkī. ジャッキー。

461. License plate. Nambā (OR: Bangō fuda). ナンバー（番号札）.

462. Light. Raito. ライト。

463. Light bulb. Denkyū. 電球。

464. Headlight. Heddo raito. ヘッド・ライト。

465. Parking light. Chūsha tō. 駐車燈。

466. Stop light. Sutoppu raito. ストップ・ライト。

467. Tailight. Tēru raito. テール・ライト。

468. Rear-view mirror. Bakku mirā. バック・ミラー。

469. Side-view mirror. Saido mirā. サイド・ミラー。

470. Motor. Mōtā. モーター。

471. Muffler. Mafurā. マフラー。

472. Nail. Kugi. 釘。

473. Nut. · Natto. ナット。

474. Oil. Oiru. オイル。

475. Pedal. Pedaru. ペダル。

476. Pliers. Puraiyā (OR: Yattoko).
プライヤー (鋏)。

477. Radiator. Rajiētā. ラジエーター。

478. Radio. Rajio. ラジオ。

479. Rags. Zōkin. 雑巾。

480. Rope. Nawa. 縄。

481. Screw. Neji. ねじ。

482. Screwdriver. Neji mawashi. ねじ回し。

483. Shock absorber. Shokku abusōbā.
ショック・アブソーバー。

484. Skid chains. Chēn. チェーン。

485. Snow tires. Sunō taiya. スノー・タイヤ 。

486. Spark plugs. Tenka puragu. 点火プラグ 。

487. Speedometer. Sokudokei. 速度計 。

488. Spring. Supuringu. スプリング 。

489. Starter. Sutātā. スターター 。

490. Steering wheel. Handoru. ハンドル 。

491. Tank. Tanku. タンク 。

492. Tire. Taiya. タイヤ 。

493. Spare tire. Supeya taiya. スペヤ・タイヤ 。

494. Tubeless tire. Chūbu nashi no taiya.
チューブ無しのタイヤ 。

495. Tire pump. Kūki ire. 空気入れ 。

496. Tools. Dōgu. 道具 。

497. Automatic transmission. Nō kuratchi.
ノー・クラッチ 。

498. Trunk. Toranku. トランク 。

499. Valve. Barubu. バルブ 。

500. Water-cooling system. Mizu reikyaku sōchi.
水冷却装置 。

501. Front wheel. Mae no sharin. 前の車輪 。

502. Rear wheel. Ushiro no sharin. 後の車輪。

503. Windshield wiper. Waipā. ワイパー。

504. Wrench. Renchi. レンチ。

MAIL

505. Where is [the post office]?
[Yūbinkyoku] wa doko desu ka?
［郵便局］は どこ で す か？

506. —a mailbox. Posuto—. ポスト―。

507. To which window should I go?
Dono madoguchi ni ikeba ii desu ka?
どの 窓口 に 行けば い ゝ で す か？

508. I want to send this letter [by surface mail].
Kono tegami o [futsūbin de] dashitai no desu ga.
この 手紙 を ［普通便 で］ 出したい の で す が。

509. —by airmail. —kōkūbin de. —航空便 で。

510. —by special delivery. —sokutatsubin de.
—速達便 で。

511. —by registered mail. —kakitome yūbin de.
—書留郵便 で。

512. I want to send this [by parcel post].
Kore o [kozutsumi yūbin de] dashitai no desu ga.
これ を［小包郵便 で］出したい の で す が。

513. How much postage do I need for this [postcard]?
Kono [hagaki] ni wa ikura no kitte ga irimasu ka?
この[葉書]には いくらの切手がいりますか？

514. The package contains [printed matter].
Kono tsutsumi ni wa [insatsubutsu] ga haitte imasu.
この包には[印刷物]が入っています。

515. —fragile material. —kowaremono.
一 壊れ物。

516. I want to insure this for [5,000 yen].
Kore ni [gosen en] no yūbimbutsu hoken o kaketai no
  desu.
ンれに[五千円]の郵便物保険をかけたいのです。

517. Give me a receipt. Uketorishō o kudasai.
受取証を下さい。

518. Will it go out [today]? [Kyō] demasu ka?
[今日] 出ますか？

519. Give me ten [ten yen] stamps.
[Jū en] no kitte o jūmai kudasai.
[十円]の切手を十枚下さい。

520. Where can I get a postal money order?
Yūbingawase no uketsuke wa doko desu ka?
郵便為替の受付けはどこですか？

521. Please forward my mail to [the Hotel Okura].
Watakushi no yūbimbutsu wa [Hoteru Ōkura] e tensō
  shite kudasai.
私の郵便物は[ホテル・オークラ]へ転送し下さい。

522. The American Express office will hold my mail.
Amerikan Ekisupuresu de yūbimbutsu o hokan shimasu.
アメリカン・エキスプレスで郵便物を保管します。

TELEGRAM

523. I would like to send [a telegram].
[Dempō] o uchitai no desu ga.
［電報］を打ちたいのびすが。

524. —a night letter. Yakan kansō dempō—.
夜間閒送電報一。

525. —a cablegram. Kaigai denshin—.
海外電信一。

526. What is the rate per word? Ichiji ikura desu ka?
一字いくらびすか？

527. What is the minimum charge?
Dempōryō wa saitei ikura desu ka?
電報料は最低いくらびすか？

528. When will an ordinary cablegram reach [New York]?
Kaigai denshin de [Nyū Yōku] ni itsu todokimasu ka?
海外電信び［ニュー・ヨーク］にいつ届きますか？

TELEPHONE

529. I would like to use the telephone.
Denwa o tsukaitai no desu ga.
電話を使いたいのびすが。

530. Would you dial this number for me?
Kono bangō e kakete kudasaimasen ka?
この番号へ かけて下さいませんか?

531. Operator, get me this number.
Moshimoshi, kono bangō o negaimasu.
もしもし、この番号を願います。

532. Call me at this number.
Kono bangō e denwa shite kudasai.
この番号へ電話して下さい。

533. My telephone number is [415-2540].
Watakushi no denwa bangō wa [yon-ichi-go no ni-go-yon-zero] desu.
私の電話番号は[四・一・五の二・五・四・ゼロ]です。

534. How much is a long-distance call to [London]?
[Rondon] e no chōkyori denwaryō wa ikura desu ka?
[ロンドン]への長距離電話料はいくらですか?

535. What is the charge for the first three minutes?
Hajime no sampunkan wa ikura desu ka?
初めの三分間はいくらですか?

536. I want to reverse the charges.
Sempōbarai ni shite hoshii no desu ga.
先方払いにして欲しいのですが。

537. Please bill me at my home phone number.
Okanjō wa jitaku no hō e tsuke ni shite kudasai.
お勘定は自宅の方へ付けにして下さい。

538. They do not answer.   Henji ga arimasen.
返事がありません。

539. The line is busy.   Hanashichū desu.
話し中です。

540. Hello (on the telephone).   Moshimoshi.
もしもし。

541. You have given me the wrong number.
Bangō ga chigatte imashita. 番号が違っいました。

542. This is [Nakano] speaking.
Kochira wa [Nakano] desu. こちらは［中野］です。

543. With whom do you want to speak?
Donata o yobidashimashō ka?
どなたを呼び出しましょうか？

544. Hold the line.   Chotto matte kudasai.
ちょっと待って下さい。

545. Dial again, please.   Kakenaoshite kudasai.
かけ直して下さい。

546. I cannot hear you.   Yoku kikoemasen.
よく聞こえません。

547. The connection is poor.   Denwa ga tōi desu.
電話が遠いです。

548. Speak louder.   Mō sukoshi ōgoe de.
もう少し大声で。

549. Call her to the phone.
Kanojo o yobidashite kudasai.
彼女を呼び出して下さい。

550. He is not here.   Kare wa orimasen.
彼は居りません。

551. You are wanted on the telephone. Odenwa desu.
お電話です。

552. May I leave a message?
Kotozuke o negaemasu ka? 言付けを願えますか？

553. Call me back. Odenwa negaimasu.
お電話願います。

554. I will call back later. Ato kara mata kakemasu.
後から又かけます。

555. I will wait for your call until [eight o'clock].
[Hachiji] made odenwa o matte imasu.
[八時] までお電話を待っています。

HOTEL

556. I am looking for [a good hotel].
[Ii hoteru] o sagashite iru no desu ga.
[いゝホテル] を捜しいるのですが。

557. —the best hotel. Ichiban ii hoteru—.
一番いゝホテル—。

558. —an inexpensive hotel. Amari takakunai hoteru—.
余り高くないホテル—。

559. —a boarding house. Geshukuya—. 下宿屋—。

560. —a Japanese inn. Ryokan—. 旅館—。

561. I want to be in [the center of town].
[Machi no chūō] ni itai no desu ga.
[町の中央] にいたいのですが。

562. I am looking for [a quiet location].
[Shizuka na tokoro] o sagashite imasu.
［静かな所］を捜しています。

563. I prefer to be close to [the university].
[Daigaku] ni chikai hō ga kekkō desu.
［大学］に近い方が結構です。

564. Do you have a vacancy?   Heya ga aite imasu ka?
部屋があいていますか？

565. I have a reservation [for tonight].
[Kon-ya no] yoyaku ga shite arimasu.
［今夜の］予約がしてあります。

566. Where is the registration desk?
Uketsuke wa doko desu ka?
受付はどこですか？

567. Fill out this registration form.
Kono yōshi ni kinyū shite kudasai.
この用紙に記入して下さい。

568. Sign here, please.   Koko e sain negaimasu.
こゝへ サイン願います。

569. Do you have [a single room]?
[Hitoribeya] ga arimasu ka?
［一人部屋］がありますか？

570. —an air-conditioned room.
Reibō no shite aru heya—. 冷房のしてある部屋ー。

571. —a quiet room.   Shizuka na heya—.
静かな部屋ー。

572. —an inside room. Uchigawa no heya—.
内側の部屋ー。

573. —an outside room. Sotomuki no heya—.
外向の部屋ー。

574. —a room with a pretty view. Keshiki no ii heya—.
景色のいゝ部屋ー。

575. I want a room [with a double bed].
[Daburu beddo] no aru heya ga hoshii no desu ga.
[ダブル・ベッド]のある部屋が欲しいのですが。

576. —with twin beds. Tsui no beddo—.
対のベッドー。

577. I want a room with [a bath].
[Basu-tsuki] no heya ga hoshii no desu ga.
[バス付き]の部屋が欲しいのですが。

578. —with a shower. Shawa-tsuki—. シャワ付きー。

579. —with television. Terebi-tsuki.— テレビ付きー。

580. I shall take a room [for one night].
[Hitoban] tomarimasu. [一晩]泊ります。

581. —for several days. Sūjitsu—. 数日ー。

582. —for a week or so. Isshūkan gurai—.
一週間位ー。

583. —for two persons. Futari—. 二人ー。

584. Can I have it [with meals]?
[Shokujitsuki] desu ka? [食事付き]ですか？

585. —**without meals.** Shokujinashi—. 食事無し一。

586. —**with breakfast only.** Asa gohan dake—.
朝ご飯だけ一。

587. What is the rate [per night]?
[Ippaku] ikura desu ka? [一泊]いくらですか？

588. —**per week.** Isshūkan—. 一週間一。

589. —**per month.** Hitotsuki—. 一月一。

590. Are tax and service charge included?
Kansetsuzei to sābisuryō wa haitte imasu ka?
間接税とサービス料は入っていますか？

591. I should like to see the room.
Heya o mitai no desu ga. 部屋を見たいのですが。

592. Don't you have something [better]?
Mō sukoshi [ii] no wa arimasen ka?
もう少し[いゝ]のはありませんか？

593. —**cheaper.** —yasui. 一安い。

594. —**larger.** —ōkii. 一大きい。

595. —**smaller.** —chiisai. 一小さい。

596. —**on a [lower] [higher] floor.**
—[shita] [ue] no kai. 一[下][上]の階。

597. —**with more light.** —akarui. 一明るい。

598. Is there a room with a view of the sea?
Umi no keshiki no mieru heya wa arimasen ka?
海の景色の見える部屋はありませんか？

599. It's too noisy. Yakamashi sugimasu.

喧し過ぎます。

600. This is satisfactory. Kore de kekkō desu.

これで結構です。

601. Is there [an elevator]? [Erebētā] wa arimasu ka?

[エレベーター]はありますか？

602. Is it [upstairs] [downstairs]?
[Nikai] [Shita] desu ka? [二階][下]ですか？

603. What is my room number?
Heya wa namban desu ka? 部屋は何番ですか？

604. Give me the room [key]. Heya no [kagi] o kudasai.

部屋の[鍵]を下さい。

605. Bring the luggage upstairs.
Nimotsu o ue e motte kite kudasai.

荷物を上へ持って来て下さい。

606. Tell the chambermaid to get my room ready.
Jochū-san ni heya o katazukeru yō ni itte kudasai.

女中さんに部屋を片付ける様に言って下さい。

607. Wake me at [eight in the morning].
[Gozen hachiji] ni okoshite kudasai.

[午前八時]に起こして下さい。

608. Do not disturb me until then.
Sore made nanimo toritsuganaide kudasai.

それまで何も取次がないで下さい。

609. I would like [breakfast] in my room.
[Asa gohan] wa heya de toritai no desu ga.

[朝ご飯]は部屋で取りたいのですが。

610. Room service, please. Rūmu sābisu o negaimasu.

ルーム・サービスを願います。

611. Please bring me [some ice].
[Kōri] o motte kite kudasai.

[氷]を持って来て下さい。

612. I want to speak to [the manager].
[Shihainin] ni hanashitai no desu ga.

[支配人]に話したいのですが。

613. Have you [a letter] for me?
Watakushi ate no [tegami] wa arimasen ka?

私宛の[手紙]はありませんか?

614. —a message. —kotozuke. 一言付け。

615. —a parcel. —kozutsumi. 一小包。

616. Send [a chambermaid].
[Jochū-san] o yokoshite kudasai.

[女中さん]をよこして下さい。

617. —a bellhop (OR: a porter). Bōi-san—.

ボーイさん一。

618. —a waiter. Wētā—. ウェーター 一。

619. —a messenger. Messenjā—. メッセンジャー一。

620. —a pageboy. Pēji-san—. ページさん一。

621. I am expecting [a friend] [a telephone call].
[Tomodachi] [Denwa] o matte iru no desu.

[友達][電話]を待っているのです。

622. Has anyone called?   Dare ka kimashita ka?

誰か来ましたか？

623. Has anyone called (by telephone)?
Denwa ga arimashita ka? 電話がありましたか？

624. Show him (OR: her) up.   Ue e annai shite kudasai.

上へ案内して下さい。

625. I shall not eat [lunch] here.
[Chūshoku] wa koko de torimasen.

［昼食］はここで取ります。

626. May I leave [these valuables] in the hotel safe?
[Kono jūyōhin] o hoteru no kinko ni irete
   moraemasu ka?

［この重要品］をホテルの金庫に入れてもらえますか？

627. I would like to get [my possessions] from the safe.
[Watakushi no azukarimono] o kinko kara dashite
   moraitai no desu.

［私の預り物］を金庫から出してもらいたいのです。

628. When must I check out?
Chekku auto wa nanji desu ka?

チェック・アウトは何時ですか？

629. I am leaving [at 10 o'clock].
Watakushi wa [jūji ni] tachimasu.

私は［十時に］立ちます。

630. Make out my bill [as soon as possible].
Kanjō o [narubeku hayaku] negaimasu.

勘定を［なるべく早く］願います。

631. Forward my mail to [Osaka].
Yūbimbutsu wa [Ōsaka] ni tensō shite kudasai.
郵便物は[大阪]に転送して下さい。

632. The cashier.   Chōba.   帳場。

633. The doorman.   Mon-ei.   門衛。

634. The lobby.   Robī.   ロビー。

HOTEL STAFF

635. The door doesn't lock.   Doa no jō ga kakarimasen.
ドアの錠がかゝりません。

636. The [toilet] is broken.   [Toire] no koshō desu.
[トイレ]の故障です。

637. The room is too [cold] [hot].
Heya ga [samu] [atsu] sugimasu.
部屋が[寒][暑]過ぎます。

638. Is this [drinking water]?
Kore wa [nomimizu] desu ka?
これは[飲み水]ですか？

639. There is no hot water.   Netsuyu ga demasen.
熱湯が出ません。

640. Wash and iron [this shirt].
[Kono shatsu] o aratte airon o kakete kudasai.
[このシャツ]を洗ってアイロンをかけて下さい。

641. Dry-clean and press [this suit].
[Kono sūtsu] o kurīningu to puresu shite kudasai.
[このスーツ]をクリーニングとプレスして下さい。

642. Bring me another [blanket].
[Mōfu] o mō ichimai motte kite kudasai.
[毛布]をもう一枚持って来て下さい。

643. Change the sheets. Shītsu o torikaete kudasai.
シーツを取替えて下さい。

644. Make the bed. Beddo o tsukutte kudasai.
ベッドを作って下さい。

645. A bath mat. Basu matto. バス・マット。

646. A bed sheet. Beddo no shītsu (OR: Shikifu).
ベッドのシーツ (敷布)。

647. A candle. Rōsoku. 蠟燭。

648. Some coathangers. Yōfukukake. 洋服掛け。

649. A pillow. Makura. 枕。

650. A pillowcase. Makura kabā. 枕カバー。

651. An adapter for electrical appliances. Hendenki.
変電機。

652. Some soap. Sekken. 石けん。

653. Some toilet paper. Toiretto pēpā. トイレット・ペーパー。

654. A towel. Taoru. タオル。

655. A wash basin. Semmenki. 洗面器。

656. A washcloth. Tenugui. 手拭。

RENTING AN APARTMENT

657. I want to rent [a furnished] [an unfurnished] apartment.
[Kagutsuki] [Kagunashi] no apāto o karitai no desu ga.
［家具付き］［家具なし］のアパートを借りたいのですが。

658. I want to rent an apartment [with a bath].
[Basutsuki (OR: Furobatsuki)] no apāto o karitai no desu ga.
［バス付き（風呂場付き）］のアパートを借りたいのですが。

659. —with two bedrooms.   Beddo rūmu futamatsuki—.
ベッド・ルーム 二間付き—。

660. —with a dining room.   Shokudōtsuki—.
食堂付き—。

661. —with a kitchen.   Daidokorotsuki—.
台所付き—。

662. Do you furnish [the linen]?
[Shītsu ya taoru-rui] wa tsuite imasu ka?
［シーツ や タオル類、］は付いていますか？

663. —the dishes.   Shokki-rui—. 食器類—。

APARTMENT: USEFUL WORDS

664. Alarm clock.   Mezamashi (OR: Mezamashidokei).
目覚まし（目覚まし時計）。

665. Ashtray.   Haizara. 灰皿。

666. Bathtub. Basu. バス。

667. Bathtub (Japanese-style). Furo. 風呂。

668. Bottle opener. Sen nuki. 栓抜き。

669. Broom. Hōki. 箒。

670. Can opener. Kankiri. 鑵切り。

671. Carpet. Jūtan. 絨毯。

672. Chair. Isu. 椅子。

673. Chest of drawers. Tansu. 箪笥。

674. Clock. Tokei. 時計。

675. Closet. Todana. 戸棚。

676. Cook. Kokku-san. コックさん。

677. Corkscrew. Koruku nuki. コルク抜き。

678. Cork (OR: Stopper). Koruku (OR: Kiruku). コルク (キルク)。

679. Curtain. Kāten. カーテン。

680. Cushion. Kusshon. クッション。

681. Cushion (Japanese style). Zabuton. 座蒲団。

682. Dishwasher. Disshu-wosshā. ディッシュ・ウオッシャー。

683. Doorbell. Beru (OR: Yobirin). ベル (呼鈴)。

684. Drapes. Dorēpusu. ドレープス。

685. Dryer. Doraiyā. ドライヤー。

686. Electric fan. Sempūki. 扇風機。

687. Fan (folding). Sensu. 扇子。

688. Fan (round). Uchiwa. 団扇。

689. Floor. Yuka. 床。

690. Housemaid. Jochū. 女中。

691. Lamp. Rampu sutando. ランプ・スタンド。

692. Light bulb. Denkyū. 電球。

693. Mirror. Kagami. 鏡。

694. Mosquito-repellent incense. Katori senkō. 蚊取り線香。

695. Mosquito net. Kaya. 蚊帳。

696. Pail. Baketsu. バケツ。

697. Rug. Shikimono. 敷き物。

698. Shower. Shawā. シャワー。

699. Sink. Nagashi. 流し。

700. Stopper. Sen. 栓。

701. Straw mat. Tatami. 畳。

702. **Table.**   Tēburu. テーブル。

703. **Tablecloth.**   Tēburukake. テーブル掛け。

704. **Terrace.**   Terasu. テラス。

705. **Tray.**   Obon (OR: Bon). お盆 (盆)。

706. **Vase.**   Kabin. 花瓶。

707. **Washing machine.**   Sentakuki. 洗濯機。

708. **Whiskbroom.**   Burashi. ブラシ。

709. **Window shades** (OR: **Venetian blinds**).   Buraindo. ブラインド。

CAFÉ AND BAR

710. **I'd like [a drink].**   [Ippai] tanomimasu. [一杯] 頼みます。

711. **—a cocktail.**   Kokkutēru—. コックテール一。

712. **—mineral water.**   Tansansui—. 炭酸水一。

713. **—a whiskey [and soda].**   Uisukī [to sōda]—. ウイスキー[とソーダ]一。

714. **—a cognac.**   Koniyakku—. コニヤック一。

715. **—a brandy.**   Burandē—. ブランデー 一。

716. **—a liqueur.**   Rikyūru—. リキュール一。

717. —gin [and tonic]. Jin [tonikku]—.
ジン [トニック] —。

718. —rum. Ramu—. ラム —。

719. —Scotch whiskey. Sukotchi uisukī—.
スコッチ・ウイスキー —。

720. —rye whiskey. Rai uisukī—. ライ・ウイスキー —。

721. —Bourbon whiskey. Burubon uisukī—.
ブルボン・ウイスキー —。

722. —vodka. Uokka—. ウオッカー —。

723. —a bottle of sake. Osake o ippon—.
お酒を一本 —。

724. —a Coca-Cola. Koka Kora—. コカコラ —。

725. —a lemonade. Remonēdo—. レモネード —。

726. —a non-alcoholic drink.
Arukōrubun no nai nomimono—.
アルコール分のない飲み物 —。

727. —beer. Bīru—. ビール —。

728. —a dark beer. Kuro bīru—. 黒ビール —。

729. —champagne. Shampen—. シャンペン —。

730. —a glass of sherry. Sherī o ippai—.
シェリーを一杯 —。

731. —red wine. Aka budōshu—. 赤葡萄酒。

732. —white wine. Shiro budōshu—.

白葡萄酒—

733. Let's have another. Mō ippai nomimashō.

もう一杯飲みましょう。

734. Cheers! (OR: Bottoms up!) Kampai! 乾杯!

RESTAURANT

735. Can you recommend a [Japanese-style restaurant]?
Yoi [Nihon no ryōriya] wa arimasen ka?

よい[日本の料理屋]はありませんか?

736. —Chinese restaurant. —Chūka ryōriya.

—中華料理屋。

737. —Western-style restaurant. —resutoran.

—レストラン。

738. —cafeteria. —kafeteria. —カフェテリア。

739. Do you have sandwiches?
Sandoitchi wa arimasu ka? サンドイッチはありますか?

740. Do you serve lunch? Hiru gohan wa dekimasu ka?

昼ご飯は出来ますか?

741. At what time is [breakfast] served?
[Asa gohan] wa nanji desu ka?

[朝ご飯]は何時ですか?

742. There are [three] of us. [Sannin] desu.

[三人]です。

743. Are you my [waiter]? Koko no [wētā] desu ka?

こゝの [ウエーター] ですか？

744. —waitress. —wētoresu.—ウェートレス。

745. I prefer a table [by the window].
Tēburu wa [madogiwa no hō] ga kekkō desu.

テーブルは [窓際の方] が結構です。

746. —in the corner. —sumi no hō. 一隅の方。

747. —outdoors. —soto no hō. 一外の方。

748. —indoors. —naka no hō. 一中の方。

749. Where is the washroom?
Toire (OR: Otearai) wa doko desu ka?

トイレ（お手洗）は どこですか？

750. We want to dine [à la carte] [table d'hôte].
[A ra karuto] [Teishoku] ni shimasu.

[ア・ラ・カルト] [定食] にします。

751. We want (to eat) something [light].
Nanika [karui] mono ni shimasu.

何か [軽い] 物に します。

752. What is the specialty of the house?
Koko no tokui no mono wa nan desu ka?

こゝの得意の物は何ですか？

753. What kind of [fish] do you have?
Donna [sakana] ga arimasu ka?

どんな [魚] がありますか？

754. Please serve us as quickly as you can.
Dekirudake isoide kudasai. 出来るだけ急いで下さい。

755. Call the bartender. Bāten o yonde kudasai.
バーテンを呼んで下さい。

756. Bring me [the menu]. [Menyū] o kudasai.
[メニュー] を下さい。

757. —the wine list. Wain risuto—. ワイン・リスト—。

758. —water. Mizu (OR: Ohiya)—. 水（お冷や）—。

759. —a napkin. Nafukin (OR: Napukin)—.
ナフキン（ナプキン）—。

760. —a hot towel.* Oshibori—. お絞り—。

761. —bread. Pan—. パン—。

762. —butter. Batā—. バター —。

763. —a cup. Kōhījawan—. コーヒー茶碗—。

764. —a fork. Hōku (OR: Fōku)—. ホーク（フォーク） —。

765. —a glass. Koppu—. コップ—。

766. —a [steak] knife. [Sutēkiyō] naifu—.
[ステーキ用] ナイフ—。

767. —a plate. Sara—. 皿 —。

768. —a large spoon. Ōsaji—. 大匙—。

* A hot, moist towel is presented to customers in Japanese restaurants (sometimes a chilled towel in hot weather).

769. —a soup spoon. Sūpuyō saji—. スープ用匙 一。

770. —a saucer. Kozara—. 小皿 一。

771. —a teaspoon. Saji—. 匙 一。

772. —chopsticks. Ohashi—. お箸 一。

773. —disposable chopsticks. Waribashi—. 割箸 一。

774. I want something [simple].
[Kantan na] mono ga hoshii no desu ga.
[簡単な]物が欲しいのですが。

775. —without meat. Niku no hairanai—.
肉の入らない 一。

776. Is it [canned]? [Kanzume] desu ka?
[罐詰]ですか?

777. —fresh. Shinsen—. 新鮮 一。

778. —frozen. Reitō—. 冷凍 一。

779. —greasy. Aburakkoi—. 脂っ濃い 一。

780. —lean. Aburakkokunai—. 脂っ濃くない 一。

781. —peppery. Peppā no aji ga tsuyoi—.
ペッパーの味が強い 一。

782. —salty. Shiokarai—. 塩辛い 一。

783. —spicy. Pirittoshita aji—. ピリッとした味 一。

784. —[very] sweet. [Taihen] amai—. [大変]甘い 一。

785. How is it prepared?   Ryōri no shikata wa?
料理の仕方は?

786. Is it [baked]?   [Ōbun de yaitamono] desu ka?
[オーブンで焼いた物]ですか?

787. —boiled.   Nitamono—. 煮た物ー。

788. —breaded.   Koromotsuki—. ころも付きー。

789. —chopped.   Kizandamono—. 刻んだ物ー。

790. —fried.   Furaimono—. フライ物ー。

791. —grilled.   Yaitamono—. 焼いた物ー。

792. —roasted.   Rōsuto shita mono—.
ローストした物ー。

793. —sautéed.   Itametamono—. 煤めた物ー。

794. —on a skewer.   Kushizashi—. 串刺しー。

795. —steamed.   Mushitamono—. 蒸した物ー。

796. —stewed.   Nitamono—. 煮た物ー。

797. This is [not fresh].   Kore wa [shinsen de wa nai].
これは[新鮮ではない]。

798. —too tough.   —kata sugimasu. ーかた過ぎます。

799. —too dry.   —kawaki sugite imasu. ー乾き過ぎています。

800. I like the meat [rare] [medium] [well-done].
Niku wa [reya] [mediamu] [weru dan] ga kekkō desu.
肉は[レヤ][メディアム][ウェル・ダン]が結構です。

801. The dish is [undercooked].
Kore wa [mada niete imasen].
これは[まだ煮えていません]。

802. —burned. —kogete imasu.—焦げています。

803. A little more. Mō sukoshi. もう少し。

804. A little less. Motto sukoshi. もっと少し。

805. Something else. Hoka no mono. ほかの物。

806. A small portion. Honno sukoshi (OR: Karuku).
ほんの少し(軽く)。

807. The next course. Tsugi no kōsu. 次のコース。

808. I have just enough. Kore de jūbun desu.
これで充分です。

809. This is dirty. Yogorete imasu. 汚れています。

810. This is too cold. Kore wa tsumeta sugimasu.
これは冷た過ぎます。

811. I did not order this. Kore wa chūmon shimasen.
これは注文しません。

812. You may take this away. Sagete kudasai.
下げて下さい。

813. May I change this for [a salad]?
Kore o [sarada] to kaeraremasu ka?
これを [サラダ] と換えうれますか？

814. What flavors do you have?
Donna aji no ga arimasu ka?
どんな味のがありますか？

815. The check, please.   Okanjō. お勘定。

816. Is the tip included?*   Chippu mo haitte imasu ka?
チップも入っていますか？

817. There is a mistake in the bill.
Kanjō ni machigai ga arimasu.
勘定に間違いがあります。

818. What are these charges for?
Kore wa nanno dai desu ka?
これは何の代ですか？

819. The food and service were excellent.
Ryōri mo sābisu mo taihen kekkō deshita.
料理もサービスも大変結構でした。

820. Hearty appetite!†   Takusan meshiagatte kudasai.
沢山召し上って下さい。

---

  * Service charge is included on all bills in Japan.
  † When one has been invited to a meal in Japan, it is proper to say *itadakimasu*, "I gratefully partake," to one's host before beginning the meal. The proper closing remark is *gochisōsama deshita*, "That was a feast."

FOOD: SPICES AND CONDIMENTS

821. Catsup. Kechappu. ケチャップ.

822. Chives. Nira. 韮.

823. Chopped flavorings. Yakumi. 薬味.

824. Dried bonito fish. Katsuobushi. 鰹節.

825. Dried bonito shavings. Hanagatsuo. 花鰹.

826. Dried seaweed. Nori. 海苔.

827. Fish stock. Dashi. 出し.

828. Garlic. Ninniku. にんにく.

829. Ginger. Shōga. 生姜.

830. Herring roe. Kazu no ko. 数の子.

831. Hot pepper. Tōgarashi. 唐辛.

832. Japanese horseradish. Wasabi. わさび.

833. Japanese pepper. Sanshō. 山椒.

834. Japanese pickles. Tsukemono. 漬物.

835. Kelp. Kombu. 昆布.

836. Mayonnaise. Mayonēzu. マヨネーズ.

837. **Molded fish paste.** Kamaboko. 蒲鉾.

838. **Monosodium glutamate.** Ajinomoto. 味の素.

839. **Mustard.** Karashi. 芥子.

840. **Pepper.** Koshō. 胡椒.

841. **Salad dressing.** Doreshingu. ドレシング.

842. **Salad oil.** Sarada yu. サラダ油.

843. **Salt.** Shio. 塩.

844. **Sauce.** Sōsu. ソース.

845. **Sesame oil.** Goma abura. 胡麻油.

846. **Sesame seeds.** Goma. 胡麻.

847. **Seven-flavor spice (a blend of spices and herbs used to garnish rice and noodle dishes).**
Shichimi-tōgarashi. 七味唐辛.

848. **Soybean paste.** Miso. 味噌.

849. **Soy sauce.** Shōyu. 醤油.

850. **Spring onions.** Naganegi. 長葱.

851. **Sugar.** Satō. 砂糖.

852. **Sweet rice wine (for cooking).** Mirin. 味醂.

853. **Trefoil (a parsley-like garnish).** Mitsuba. 三葉.

854. Vinegar. Su. 酢 .

BEVERAGES AND BREAKFAST FOODS

855. [Black] coffee. Kōhī [burakku]. コーヒー[ブラック] 。

856. Hot chocolate. Hotto kokoa. ホット・コ>ア。

857. Tea with lemon. Remon tī. レモン・ティー 。

858. Black tea [with cream] [with milk].
Kōcha [ni kurīmu] [ni miruku].
紅茶[にクリーム][にミルク]。

859. Iced [tea] [coffee]. Aisu [tī] [kōhī]. アイス[ティー][コーヒー]。

860. [Fruit] [Orange] [Tomato] juice.
[Furūtsu] [Orenji] [Tomato] jūsu.
[フルーツ][オレンジ][トマト] ジュース。

861. [Dark] [White] bread. [Kuro] [Shiro] pan.
[黒,][白] パン。

862. Coffee cake. Kōhī kēki. コーヒー・ケーキ 。

863. [Soft] [Hard] rolls. [Yawarakai] [Katai] rōru pan.
[柔らかい][かたい] ロール・パン。

864. Toast. Tōsuto. トースト。

865. Jam. Jamu. ジャム 。

866. Marmalade. Māmarēdo. マーマレード。

867. Cereal. Shiriaru. シリアル。

868. Cornflakes. Kōn furēki. コーン・フレーキ。

869. Pancakes. Pankēki. パンケーキ。

870. Hotcakes. Hottokēki. ホットケーキ。

871. Bacon [and eggs]. Bēkon [to tamago].
ベーコン[と卵]。

872. Fried eggs. Medamayaki. 目玉焼。

873. Poached eggs. Pōchi eggusu. ポーチ・エッグス。

874. Ham and eggs. Hamu eggu(su). ハム・エッグ(ス)。

875. Omelet. Omuretsu. オムレツ。

876. Soft-boiled eggs. Hanjuku tamago.
半熟玉子。

877. Hard-boiled eggs. Yude tamago. ゆで卵。

SOUPS AND SALADS

878. Chicken soup. Chikin sūpu (OR: Tori no sūpu).
チキン・スープ(鳥のスープ)。

879. Consommé. Konsome. コンソメ。

880. Tomato soup. Tomato sūpu. トマト・スープ。

881. Vegetable soup. Yasai sūpu. 野菜スープ。

882. Chicken salad. Chikin sarada. チキン・サラダ。

883. Green salad. Yasai sarada. 野菜サラダ。

884. Shrimp salad. Shurimpu sarada. シュリンプ・サラダ。

885. Lobster salad. Robusutā sarada. ロブスター・サラダ。

886. Tomato salad. Tomato sarada. トマト・サラダ。

MEATS

887. Beef. Gyūniku. 牛肉。

888. Ground beef. Hikiniku. 挽き肉。

889. Roast beef. Rōsuto bīfu. ロースト・ビーフ。

890. Croquettes. Korokke. コロッケ。

891. Cutlets. Katsuretsu. カツレツ。

892. Ham. Hamu. ハム。

893. Lamb. Kohitsuji no niku. 子羊の肉。

894. Liver. Rebā. レバー。

895. Mutton. Yōniku. 羊肉。

896. Pork. Butaniku. 豚肉。

897. Pork cutlet. Tonkatsu. 豚カツ。

898. Sausage. Sosēji. ソセージ。

899. Steak (OR: **Beefsteak**). Sutēki (OR: Bifuteki).
ステーキ（ビフテキ）。

POULTRY

900. Chicken. Toriniku (OR: Kashiwa).
鳥肉（かしわ）。

901. Chicken liver. Kimo. 肝 。

902. Duck. Kamo. 鴨 。

903. Pheasant. Kiji. 雉子。

904. Quail. Uzura. 鶉 。

905. Turkey. Tākī. ターキー。

FISH AND SEAFOOD

906. Abalone. Awabi. 鮑 。

907. Bass. Suzuki. 鱸 。

908. Blowfish. Fugu. ふぐ 。

909. Clams. Hamaguri. 虫合 。

910. Cod. Tara. 鱈 。

911. Cod roe. Tarako. 鱈子 。

912. Crab. Kani. 蟹 。

913. Eel. Unagi. 鰻 。

914. Flounder. Hirame. 比目魚 。

915. Herring. Nishin. にしん。

916. Lobster. Ise ebi. 伊勢蝦。

917. Mackerel. Saba. 鯖。

918. Octopus. Tako. 蛸。

919. Oysters. Kaki. かき。

920. Salmon. Shake (OR: Sake). 鮭。

921. Sardines. Iwashi. 鰯。

922. Scallops. Kaibashira. 貝柱。

923. Sea bream. Tai. 鯛。

924. Sea slug. Namako. なまこ。

925. Shrimp. Ebi. 海老(蝦)。

926. Snapping turtle. Suppon. すっぽん。

927. Sole. Karei. 鰈。

928. Squid. Ika. 烏賊。

929. Swordfish. Kajiki. 旗魚。

930. Trout. Masu. 鱒。

931. Freshwater trout. Ayu. 鮎。

932. Tuna. Maguro. 鮪。

933. Whale. Kujira. 鯨。

VEGETABLES

934. Asparagus. Asupara. アスパラ。

935. Bamboo shoots. Takenoko. 筍。

936. Beans. Mame. 豆。

937. Lima beans. Soramame. 蚕豆。

938. Red beans. Azuki. 小豆。

939. Soybeans. Daizu. 大豆。

940. String beans. Ingen. 隠元。

941. Bean curd. Tōfu. 豆腐。

942. Fried bean curd. Abura-age. 油揚げ。

943. Bean sprouts. Moyashi. 萌し。

944. Burdock root. Gobō. 牛蒡。

945. Cabbage. Kyabetsu. キャベツ。

946. Chinese cabbage. Hakusai. 白菜。

947. Carrots. Ninjin. 人参。

948. Chrysanthemum greens. Shungiku. 春菊。

949. Cucumbers. Kyūri. 胡瓜。

950. Eggplant. Nasu (OR: Nasubi). 茄子 (茄)。

951. Lettuce. Retasu (OR: Saradana).
レタス（サラダ菜）。

952. Lotus root. Renkon. 蓮根。

953. Mushrooms. Masshurūmu. マッシュルーム。

954. Dried mushrooms. Shiitake. 椎茸。

955. Japanese mushrooms. Matsutake. 松茸。

956. Mustard greens. Karashina. 芥子菜。

957. Okra. Okura. オクラ。

958. Onions. Tamanegi. 玉葱。

959. Peas. Endōmame. 豌豆まめ。

960. Green peppers. Pīman. ピーマン。

961. Potatoes. Jagaimo. じゃがいも。

962. Sweet potatoes. Satsuma imo. 薩摩いも。

963. Spinach. Hōrensō. 菠薐草。

964. Taro. Satoimo. 里芋。

965. Tomatoes. Tomato. トマト。

966. Turnips. Kabu (OR: Kabura). 蕪（蕪菁）。

967. Watercress. Seri. 芹。

968. White radish. Daikon. 大根。

CEREALS AND STARCHES

969. Starch paste noodles. Shirataki. 白滝 。

970. Buckwheat noodles. Soba. そば 。

971. Dumplings. Dango. 団子 。

972. Instant noodles. Ramen. ラーメン 。

973. Rice (cooked). Gohan. ご飯 。

974. Rice (uncooked). Kome. 米 。

975. Rice cakes. Mochi. 餅 。

976. Spaghetti. Supagettī. スパゲッティー 。

977. Vermicelli. Sōmen. そうめん 。

978. Wheat noodles. Udon. うどん 。

FRUITS AND NUTS

979. Apple. Ringo. 林檎 。

980. Banana. Banana. バナナ 。

981. Cherries. Sakurambo. 桜んぼ 。

982. Chestnuts. Kuri. 栗 。

983. Gingko nuts. Ginnan. 銀杏 。

984. Grapefruit. Gurēpufurūto. グレープ・フルート。

985. Grapes. Budō. 葡萄。

986. Kumquats. Kinkan. 金柑。

987. Lemon. Remon. レモン。

988. Loquats. Biwa. 枇杷。

989. Melon. Meron. メロン。

990. Orange. Orenji. オレンジ。

991. Peach. Momo (OR: Suimitsu).
桃（水蜜）。

992. Pear. Nashi. 梨。

993. Persimmon. Kaki. 柿。

994. Pineapple. Painappuru. パイナップル。

995. Plums. Sumomo. 李。

996. Strawberries. Ichigo. 苺。

997. Mandarin orange. Mikan. 蜜柑。

998. Watermelon. Suika. 西瓜。

DESSERTS

999. Cake. Kēki. ケーキ。

1000. Cookies.   Kukkī (OR: Bisuketto).
クッキー（ビスケット）。

1001. Custard.   Kasutādo. カスタード。

1002. French pastry.   Yōgashi. 洋菓子。

1003. [Vanilla] [Chocolate] ice cream.
[Banira] [Chokorēto] aisu kurīmu.
［バニラ］［チョコレート］アイス・クリーム。

1004. Pie.   Pai. パイ。

1005. Pudding.   Pudingu (OR: Puringu).
プディング（プリング）。

1006. Sherbet.   Shābetto. シャーベット。

1007. Sponge cake.   Kasutera. カステラ。

JAPANESE FOODS*

SHIRUMONO
Soups.

1008. Ebi suimono. 海老吸い物。
Clear soup with shrimp.

1009. Hamaguri ushiojiru. 蛤潮汁。
Clam consommé.

---

* The following sections form a list of typical Japanese foods, and will serve as an introduction to the outstanding and elegant Japanese cuisine. We have followed the traditional Japanese culinary categories, which are based on methods of preparation. They are presented roughly in the order of courses in a formal banquet, though both simple and more refined dishes are included here.

1010. Kaminarijiru. 雷汁.
Thunder soup (with bean curd and vegetables).

1011. Misoshiru. 味噌汁.　　　　　Soup with *miso*.

1012. Suimono (OR: **Osumashi**). 澄い物〔お澄し〕.
Clear soup with meat, chicken or fish in *dashi* stock.

1013. Zōni (OR: **Ozōni**). 雑煮.〔お雑煮.〕
Clear soup and vegetables served with New Year's rice cakes.

SASHIMI

Sliced raw fish or chicken served with garnishes of grated
　　gingerroot or Japanese horseradish and soy sauce.
1014. Karei no sashimi. 鰈の刺身.
Sliced flounder.

1015. Maguro no sashimi. 鮪の刺身.
Sliced tuna.

1016. Tai no sashimi. 鯛の刺身.　　　　Sliced sea bream.

1017. Tori no sashimi. 鳥の刺身.
Sliced raw chicken.

YAKIMONO

　　　Grilled, broiled, and pan-fried foods.
1018. Gyūniku no yawatamaki. 牛肉の八幡巻.
Beef and burdock root rolls.

1019. Kabayaki. 蒲焼.
Broiled eels basted with *sake* and soy sauce.

1020. Sakana no teriyaki. 魚の照焼.
Marinated broiled fish.

1021. Suzuki shioyaki. 鱸塩焼。
Salt-grilled sea bass.

1022. Yakitori. 焼鳥。
Pieces of chicken broiled on skewers.

1023. Yakizakana. 焼魚。。 Grilled fish.

MUSHIMONO
Steamed foods.

1024. Chawan mushi. 茶碗蒸し。
A savory custard with eggs, chicken, shrimp, gingko nuts
and vegetables steamed in individual bowls.

1025. Chiri mushi. ちり蒸し。
Steamed salmon casserole.

1026. Dobin mushi. 土瓶蒸し。
Mushroom and chicken steamed in earthenware pot.

1027. Odamaki mushi. 芋環蒸し。
Steamed noodles, eggs, fish cakes and vegetables.

1028. Sake no oyakomushi. 鮭の親子蒸し。
Steamed salmon and salmon roe.

NIMONO
Simmered foods.

1029. Nimame. 煮豆 Boiled beans.

1030. Nizakana. 煮魚。。 Simmered fish.

1031. Oden. おでん。
Stew with molded fish paste, fried fish balls, egg and
vegetables.

1032. Toriganni. 烏がん煮。   Chicken balls.

1033. Tori no nimono. 烏の煮物。
Simmered chicken and vegetables.

1034. Tsukudani. 佃煮。
Fish, shellfish and seaweed simmered with soy sauce and
    sugar.

AGEMONO
Deep-fried foods.

1035. Beinasu iridashi. 米なすいりだし。
Deep-fried eggplant.

1036. Kanidōfu iridashi. 蟹豆腐いりだし。
Crab-and-bean curd balls in broth.

1037. Karei Rikyū funamori. かれい利久舟盛り。
Flounder served in edible "boats."

1038. Nasu hasami age. 茄子はさみあげ。
Deep-fried stuffed eggplant.

1039. Tempura. てんぷら。
Seafood and vegetables dipped in batter and deep-fried,
    served with a special sauce.

1040. Toriniku tatsuta age. 烏肉たつたあげ。
Deep-fried marinated chicken.

SUNOMONO
Vegetables or seafood with vinegar dressing.
1041. Kanisu. 蟹酢。   Vinegared crab.

1042. Kōhaku namasu. 紅白なます。
Red-and-white (carrot and giant radish) vinegared salad.

1043. Kyūri no sumomi. 胡瓜の酢もみ。
Vinegared cucumber.

1044. Sudako. 酢蛸。 Vinegared octopus.

AEMONO
Dressed foods (salads).

1045. Hōrensō no goma ae. ほうれん草の胡麻あえ。
Spinach with sesame dressing.

1046. Nuta. ぬた。 Shellfish with *miso* dressing.

1047. Shirazu ae. 白酢あえ。 Tangy white salad.

1048. Tataki gobō. 叩き牛蒡。
Crushed burdock root with sesame dressing.

NABEMONO
Foods cooked at the table.

1049. Chirinabe. ちり鍋。 Fish and vegetables.

1050. Mizutaki. 水炊き。 Chicken and vegetables.

1051. Shabu-shabu. しゃぶしゃぶ。 Beef and vegetables.

1052. Sukiyaki (OR: **Gyūnabe**). すきやき（牛鍋）。
Beef and vegetables simmered in richly flavored sauce.

1053. Yosenabe. 寄せ鍋。
Meat or fish and vegetable stew.

GOHANMONO
Rice dishes.

1054. Okowa (OR: **Osekihan**). お強（お赤飯）。
Rice boiled with red beans.

1055. Oyako domburi. 親子丼.
Chicken, eggs and vegetables over rice.

1056. Taimeshi. 鯛飯 .   Rice boiled with sea bream.

1057. Takenokomeshi. 筍飯.
Rice boiled with bamboo shoots.

1058. Tendon. 天丼.   Shrimp *tempura* over rice.

1059. Unagi domburi. 鰻丼.
Broiled eels over rice.

SUSHI
Vinegared rice with fish or other ingredients.
1060. Chirashizushi. 散らし鮨.
Rice mixed with eggs, mushrooms and chopped vegetables.

1061. Inarizushi. 稲荷鮨.
Rice balls wrapped in fried bean curd.

1062. Norimaki (OR: **Makizushi**). 海苔巻き
(巻き鮨)
Rice rolled in seaweed, stuffed with egg, spinach or other
    ingredients.

1063. Sushi (OR: **Nigirizushi**). 鮨(寿司) (握り鮨).
Hand-shaped ovals of vinegared rice topped with Japanese
    horseradish and a slice of raw fish, seafood or egg.

MENRUI
Noodle dishes.
1064. Hiyamugi. 冷や麦.
Cold noodles served with a sweet soy-sauce dip.

1065. Kakesoba. かけ蕎麦.
Buckwheat noodles in broth.

1066. Kamo namban. 鴨南ばん。
Duck with vermicelli served in soup.

1067. Okame soba. おかめ蕎麦。
Buckwheat noodles with slices of molded fish paste and
  other ingredients served in broth.

1068. Tempura soba. てんぷら蕎麦。
Shrimp *tempura* over buckwheat noodles in broth.

TSUKEMONO
Pickled vegetables.

1069. Benishōga. 紅生姜。   Pickled red ginger.

1070. Fukujinzuke. 福神漬。
Sliced vegetables pickled in soy sauce.

1071. Hakusai no shiozuke. 白菜の塩漬。
Chinese cabbage pickled in salt.

1072. Narazuke. 奈良漬。
Gourd or other vegetables pickled in the lees of *sake*.

1073. Shiozuke. 塩漬。   Vegetables pickled in salt.

1074. Suzuke. 酢漬け。   Vegetables pickled in vinegar.

1075. Takuan. 沢庵。
Dried giant radish pickled in brine.

1076. Umeboshi. 梅干。   Pickled sour plums.

OKASHI
Sweets and confections.

1077. Higashi. 干菓子。 Dry confections.

1078. Kakimochi. かき餅。
Small cookies or crackers with soy-sauce flavoring.

1079. Manjū (OR: **Omanjū**). 饅頭 (お饅頭)。
Rice-flour cakes stuffed with sweet bean paste.

1080. Mitsumame. 蜜豆。
Gelatin cubes and boiled sweet beans and fruit in syrup.

1081. Mushigashi. 蒸菓子。 Steamed rice-flour cake.

1082. Ohagi. お萩。
Confection made of glutinous rice and sweet bean paste.

1083. Sakuramochi. 桜餅。
Bean-paste cake wrapped in cherry leaf.

1084. Sembei (OR: **Osembei**). 煎餅 (お煎餅)。
Rice crackers.

1085. Shio sembei. 塩煎餅。
Rice crackers flavored with soy sauce.

1086. Shiruko (OR: **Oshiruko**). 汁粉 (おしるこ)。
Sweet red bean soup with dumplings or rice cakes.

1087. Yōkan. 羊羹。 Molded bean-paste cakes.

NOMIMONO
Beverages.

1088. Bancha. 番茶。 Coarse green tea.

1089. Gyokuro. 玉露。   Superior green tea.

1090. Matcha. 抹茶。
Powdered green tea (used in tea ceremony).

1091. Ocha (OR: **Cha**). お茶 (茶)。
Japanese green tea.

1092. Sencha. 煎茶。   Medium-grade green tea.

1093. Toso (OR: **Otoso**). 屠蘇 (おとそ)。
Sweet *sake* and herbs, served on New Year's day.

1094. Usucha. 薄茶。   Weak powdered tea.

SIGHTSEEING

1095. I would like a guide [who speaks English].
[Eigo no dekiru] gaido ga hoshii no desu ga.
[英語の出来る]ガイドが欲しいのですが。

1096. How long will [the excursion] take?
[Yūran] wa nanjikan kakarimasu ka?
[遊覧]は何時間かかりますか？

1097. Must I book in advance?
Maemotte yoyaku suru no desu ka?
前以つて予約するのですか？

1098. Are admission tickets and lunch included?
Nyūjōken to chūshoku no daikin wa fukumarete imasu ka?
入場券と昼食の代金は含まれていますか？

1099. What is the charge (for a trip) [to the island]?
[Shima made] ikura desu ka?
[島まで]いくらですか？

1100. —to the mountain.　Yama made—.　山まで―。

1101. —to the sea.　Umibe made—.　海辺まで―。

1102. —around the city.　Machi o isshū shitara—.
町を一周したら―。

1103. —to the suburbs (OR: outskirts).　Kinkō made—.
近郊まで―。

1104. Call for me [tomorrow] at my hotel at 8 A.M.
[Myōnichi] gozen hachiji ni hoteru e mukae ni kite kudasai.
［明日］午前八時にホテルへ迎えに来て下さい。

1105. Show me the sights of interest.
Omo na meisho o misete kudasai.
主な名所を見せて下さい。

1106. What is [that building]?
[Ano tatemono] wa nan desu ka?
［あの建物］は何ですか？

1107. How old is it?　Dono kurai furui no desu ka?
どの位古いのですか？

1108. Can we go in?　Hairemasu ka?　入れますか？

1109. I am interested in [architecture].
Watakushi wa [kenchiku] ni kyōmi ga arimasu.
私は［建築］に興味があります。

1110. —archeology.　—kōkogaku.　―考古学。

1111. —sculpture.　—chōkoku.　―彫刻。

1112. —painting.　—kaiga.　―繪画。

1113. —design. —dezain. 一デザイン。

1114. —native arts and crafts. —mingei ya kōgei.
一民芸や工芸。

1115. —modern art. —kindai bijutsu. 一近代美術。

1116. I should like to see [the park].
[Kōen] ga mitai no desu ga. [公園] が見たいのですが。

1117. —the cathedral. Kyōkai—. 教会一。

1118. —the library. Toshokan—. 図書館一。

1119. —the palace. Goten—. 御殿一。

1120. —the castle. Shiro—. 城一。

1121. —the museum. Hakubutsukan—. 博物館一。

1122. —the zoo. Dōbutsuen—. 動物園一。

1123. Let's go see [the landscaped garden].
[Teien] o mi ni yukimashō. [庭園] を見に行きましょう。

1124. A beautiful view! Utsukushii keshiki!
美しい景色!

1125. Very interesting! Hijō ni omoshiroi!
非常に面白い!

1126. Magnificent! Subarashii! 素晴らしい!

1127. We are enjoying ourselves.
Kekkō tanoshinde imasu. 結構楽しんでいます。

1128. I am bored.　Taikutsu desu. 退屈です。

1129. When does the museum [open] [close]?
Hakubutsukan wa itsu [akimasu] [shimarimasu] ka?
博物館はいつ[開きます][締まります]か?

1130. Is this the way to the [entrance] [exit]?
[Iriguchi] [Deguchi] wa kochira desu ka?
[入口][出口]はこちらですか?

1131. Let's visit the [fine arts gallery].
[Bijutsukan] ni mairimashō. [美術館]に参りましょう。

1132. Let's stay longer.　Mō sukoshi nagaku imashō.
もう少し長くいましょう。

1133. Let's leave now.　Demashō. 出ましょう。

1134. We must be back by 5 o'clock.
Goji made ni modoranakereba narimasen.
五時までに戻らなければなりません。

1135. If there is time, let's rest a while.
Jikan ga areba chotto yasumimashō.
時間があればちょっと休みましょう。

WORSHIP

1136. Altar.　Saidan. 祭壇。

1137. Buddhist temple.　Otera (OR: Tera).
お寺(寺)。

1138. Catholic church.　Katorikku kyōkai.
カトリック教会。

1139. Church music. Kyōkai ongaku. 教会音楽。

1140. Collection. Kenkin. 献金。

1141. Communion. Seizan haiju. 聖ざん拝受。

1142. Confession. Kokuhaku. 告白。

1143. Contribution. Kifu. 寄付。

1144. Mass. Misa. ミサ。

1145. Minister. Bokushi. 牧師。

1146. Offering (OR: **Offertory**). Saisen. 賽銭。

1147. Prayers. Kitō. 祈とう。

1148. Shinto prayers. Norito. 祝詞。

1149. Prayer book. Kitōsho. 祈とう書。

1150. Priest. Shimpu (OR: Shimpusan).
神父（神父さん）。

1151. Buddhist priest. Obōsan (OR: Bōzu).
お坊さん（坊主）。

1152. Shinto priest. Kannushi. 神主。

1153. Protestant church.
Purotesutanto (OR: Shinkyō no) kyōkai.
プロテスタント（新教の）教会。

1154. Rabbi. Rabai. ラバイ。

1155. Sermon.   Sekkyō.   説教。

1156. Services.   Reihai.   礼拝。

1157. Shinto shrine.   Jinja.   神社。

1158. Sunday school.   Nichiyō gakkō. 日曜学校。

1159. Sutra (Buddhist scripture).   Okyō. お経。

1160. Synagogue.   Yudaya kyōkai. ユダヤ教会。

ENTERTAINMENTS

1161. Is there [a matinée] today?
Kyō wa [machinē] ga arimasu ka?
今日は［マチネー］がありますか？

1162. Has [the show] begun?
[Shibai] wa mō hajimarimashita ka?
［芝居］はもう始まりましたか？

1163. What is playing now?   Nani o jōenshite imasu ka?
何を上演していますか？

1164. Have you any seats for tonight?
Komban no ken wa arimasu ka?
今晩の券はありますか？

1165. How much is [an orchestra seat]?
[Ikkai seki] wa ikura desu ka?
［一階席］はいくらですか？

1166. —a balcony seat.   Nikai seki—. 二階席ー。

1167. —a reserved seat. Shitei seki—. 指定席一。

1168. Not too far from the stage.
Butai kara amari tōkunai tokoro.
舞台から余り遠くない所。

1169. Here is my [ticket stub].
Kore ga [ken no hikae] desu. これが [券の控え] です。

1170. Can I [see] [hear] well from there?
Soko wa yoku [miemasu] [kikoemasu] ka?
そこはよく [見えます] [聞こえます] か？

1171. When does the program start? (LIT.: When does the curtain go up?)
Maku wa itsu akimasu ka? 幕はいつ明きますか？

1172. How long is the intermission?
Kyūkei wa dono kurai desu ka?
休憩はどの位ですか？

1173. When does the show [begin] [end]?
Itsu [hajimarimasu] [owarimasu] ka?
いつ [始まります] [終ります] か？

1174. Everyone enjoyed the show. Mina tanoshimimashita.
みな楽しみました。

1175. The ballet. Barē. バレー。

1176. The box office. Kippu uriba. 切符売場。

1177. The circus. Sākasu. サーカス。

1178. The concert. Ongakukai (OR: Ongakkai). 音楽会。

1179. The folk dances.   Kyōdo buyō. 郷土舞踊.

1180. The Kabuki theater.   Kabuki. 歌舞伎.

1181. The [beginning] [end] of the line.
Retsu no [hajime] [owari]. 列の[始め][終り].

1182. The movies.   Eiga. 映画.

1183. The musical comedy.   Myūjikaru komedī.
ミュージカル・コメディー.

1184. The nightclub.   Naito kurabu (OR: Kyabarē).
ナイト・クラブ (キャバレー).

1185. The Nō theater.   Onō. お能.

1186. The opera.   Opera. オペラ.

1187. The opera glasses.   Opera gurasu. オペラ・グラス.

1188. The program (booklet).   Puroguramu (OR: Bangumi).
プログラム (番組).

1189. The puppet show.   Bunraku (OR: Ningyō shibai).
文楽 (人形芝居).

1190. The sports event.   Supōtsu kyōgi. スポーツ競技.

1191. Standing room.   Tachimi. 立見.

1192. The theater.   Gekijō. 劇場.

1193. The movie theater.   Eigakan. 映画館.

NIGHTCLUB AND DANCING

1194. How much is [the admission charge]?
[Nyūjōryō] wa ikura desu ka?
[入場料]はいくらですか？

1195. Is there a floor show?   Furoa shō wa arimasu ka?
フロア・ショー はありますか？

1196. Where can we go to dance?
Dansu wa doko de dekimasu ka?
ダンスはどこで出来ますか？

1197. May I have this dance?
Kono dansu onegai dekimasu ka?
このダンスお願い出来ますか？

1198. You dance very well.   Dansu wa nakanaka ojōzu desu.
ダンスは中々お上手です。

1199. Will you play a [rumba]?   [Rumba] o negaimasu.
[ルンバ]を願います。

1200. —a samba.   Samba—.   サンバー。

1201. —a tango.   Tango—.   タンゴー。

1202. —a waltz.   Warutsu—.   ワルツー。

1203. —country music.   Kantorī—.   カントリーー。

1204. —jazz.   Jazu—.   ジャズー。

1205. —rock music.   Rokku—.   ロックー。

1206. The discotheque.   Disuko.   ディスコ。

SPORTS AND GAMES

1207. We want to play [cards].
[Torampu] o shitai no desu ga.
[トランプ] をしたい のですが。

1208. —golf. Gorufu—. ゴルフ ー。

1209. —mahjong. Mājan—. 麻雀 ー。

1210. —ping-pong. Pinpon—. ピンポン ー。

1211. —tennis. Tenisu—. テニス ー。

1212. We want to watch [baseball].
[Yakyū] o mitai no desu ga. [野球] を見たい のですが

1213. —basketball. Basuketto (bōru)—.
バスケット (ボール) ー。

1214. —rugby. Ragubī—. ラグビー ー。

1215. —volleyball. Barēbōru—. バレーボール ー。

1216. —wrestling. Sumō—. 相撲 ー。

1217. We want to go bowling. Bōringu o shitai no desu ga.
ボーリング をしたい のですが。

1218. Do you play [chess]? [Chesu] o saremasu ka?
[チェス] をされますか？

1219. —checkers. Chekkā—. チェッカー ー。

1220. —Japanese chess. Go—. 碁 ー。

1221. —bridge. Burijji—. ブリッジ ー。

1222. Let's go swimming.   Oyogi ni ikimashō.
泳ぎに いきましよう。

1223. Let's go to [the swimming pool].
[Pūru] ni ikimashō. [プール]に いきましよう。

1224. —the beach.   Kaigan—.   海岸—。

1225. —the horse races.   Keiba—.   競馬—。

1226. —the skating rink.   Sukētojō—.   スケート場—。

1227. I need [golf equipment].
[Gorufu no dōgu] ga irimasu. [ゴルフの道具]が要ります。

1228. —fishing tackle.   Tsuri dōgu—.   釣り道具—。

1229. —a tennis racket.   Raketto—.   ラケット—。

1230. Shall we go [fishing]?   [Sakanatsuri] ni ikimashō ka?
[魚つり]に いきましようか。?

1231. —horseback riding.   Umanori—.   馬乗リ—。

1232. —roller skating.   Rōrā sukēto.   ローラー・スケート—。

1233. —ice skating.   Aisu sukēto—.   アイス・スケート—。

1234. —skiing.   Sukī—.   スキー —。

HIKING AND CAMPING

1235. How long a walk is it to the [hostel]?
[Hosuteru] made aruite dono kurai desu ka?
[ホステル]まで 歩いて どの 位 ですか?

1236. Let's go camping.   Kyampingu ni mairimashō.
キャンピングに参りましよう。

1237. Are sanitary facilities available?
Semmenjo-nado no setsubi wa arimasu ka?
洗面所等の設備はありますか?

1238. Campsite.   Kyampujō.   キャンプ場。

1239. Camping equipment.   Kyampu yōhin.
キャンプ用品。

1240. Camping permit.   Kyampuyō kyoka.
キャンプ用許可。

1241. Cooking utensils.   Kyampuyō shokkirui.
キャンプ用食器類。

1242. Campfire.   Kyampu faiyā. キャンプ・ファイヤー。

1243. Firewood.   Takigi. 薪。

1244. Footpath.   Komichi. 小路。

1245. Hike.   Haiku. ハイク。

1246. Matches.   Matchi. マッチ。

1247. Picnic.   Pikunikku. ピクニック。

1248. Rubbish.   Gomi. ごみ。

1249. Rubbish receptacle.   Gomibako. ごみ箱。

1250. Shortcut.   Chikamichi. 近道。

1251. Tent. Tento. テント。

1252. Thermos. Mahōbin. 魔法びん。

1253. Drinking water. Nomimizu. 飲み水。

1254. Woods. Hayashi. 林。

1255. Forest. Mori (OR: Shinrin). 森 (森林)。

1256. Lake. Mizuumi. 湖。

1257. Mountain. Yama. 山。

1258. Pond. Ike. 池。

1259. River. Kawa. 川 (河)。

1260. Stream. Ogawa. 小川。

BANK AND MONEY

1261. Where can I change money?
Doko de ryōgae ga dekimashō ka?
どこで両替えが出来ましようか？

1262. What is the exchange rate on the [dollar] [pound]?
[Doru] [Pondo] no kawase sōba wa ikura deshō ka?
[ドル] [ポンド] の為替相場は いくらでしようか？

1263. Where is the [bank]? [Ginkō] wa doko deshō ka?
[銀行] はどこでしようか？

1264. Will you cash [a personal check]?
[Kogitte] o kaete moraemasu ka?
[小切手] を替えてもらえますか？

1265. —a traveler's check.   Toraberā chekku—.
トラベラー・チェック—。

1266. I have [a bank draft].   [Ginkō tegata] ga arimasu.
[銀行手形] がありま す。

1267. —a letter of credit.   Shin-yōjō—.   信用状—。

1268. —a credit card.   Kurejitto kādo—.
クレジット・カード—。

1269. I would like to exchange [twenty] dollars.
[Nijū] doru kaetai no desu ga.
[二十] ドル替えたい のですが。

1270. Please give me [large bills].   [Ōkii satsu] o kudasai.
[大きい札] を下さい。

1271. —small bills.   Chiisai satsu—.   小さい札—。

1272. —small change.   Komakai no—.   細かいの—。

SHOPPING

1273. Show me [the hat] in the window.
Shōkēsu ni aru [bōshi] o misete kudasai.
ショー・ケース にある[帽子] を見せて下さい。

1274. Can you help me?   Chotto onegai dekimasu ka?
ちょっとお願い出来ますか?

1275. I am just looking around.   Mite iru dake desu.
見ているだけです。

1276. I shall come back later. Mata ato kara kimasu.
又後から来ます。

1277. I've been waiting [a long time].
[Nagai koto] matte imashita.
[長いこと] 待っていました。

1278. What brand do you have?
Donna burando no ga arimasu ka?
どんなブランドのがありますか？

1279. How much is this? Kore wa ikura desu ka?
これはいくらですか？

1280. How much [per piece]? [Ikko] ikura desu ka?
[一箇] いくらですか？

1281. —per meter. Ichi mētoru—. 一メートル一。

1282. —per gram. Ichi guramu—. 一グラム一。

1283. —per kilo. Ichi kiro—. 一キロ一。

1284. —per package. Hito tsutsumi—. 一包み一。

1285. —per bunch. Hito taba—. 一束一。

1286. —all together. Zembu de—. 全部で一。

1287. It is too expensive. Taka sugimasu.
高過ぎます。

1288. It is [cheap]. [Yasui] desu. [安い] です。

1289. —reasonable. Tegoro na nedan—.
手頃な値段 一。

1290. Is that your lowest price?
Sore ga ichiban yasui nedan desu ka?
それが一番安い値段ですか？

1291. Do you allow a discount?   Waribiki shimasu ka?
割引しますか？

1292. I do not like that.   Sore wa ki ni irimasen.
それは気に入りません。

1293. Don't you have something [better]?
[Mō sukoshi ii] no wa arimasen ka?
［もう少しいゝ］のはありませんか？

1294. —cheaper.   Mō sukoshi yasui—.
もう少し安い一。

1295. —more stylish.   Motto ii sutairu—.
もっといゝスタイル一。

1296. —softer.   Mō sukoshi yawarakai—.
もう少し柔らかい一。

1297. —stronger.   Mō sukoshi jōbu na—.
もう少し丈夫な一。

1298. —heavier.   Mō sukoshi atsubottai—.
もう少し厚ぼったい一。

1299. —lighter (in weight).   Mō sukoshi karui—.
もう少し軽い一。

1300. —tighter.   Mō sukoshi kitsui—.
もう少しきつい一。

1301. —looser.   Mō sukoshi yurui—.
もう少しゆるい一。

1302. —lighter (in color). Mō sukoshi usui iro—.
もう少し薄い色 —。

1303. —darker. Mō sukoshi koi iro—.
もう少し濃い色 —。

1304. Do you have this in [my size]?
[Watakushi no saizu] no ga arimasu ka?
[私のサイズ]のがありますか？

1305. —a larger size. Mō sukoshi ōkii—.
もう少し大きい —。

1306. —a smaller size. Mō sukoshi chiisai—.
もう少し小さい —。

1307. —another color. Hoka no iro—. 他の色 —。

1308. —a different style. Betsu no sutairu—.
別のスタイル —。

1309. Where is the fitting room?
Kitsukeshitsu wa doko desu ka?
着付け室はどこですか？

1310. May I try it on? Kite mite mo ii deshō ka?
着て見てもいゝでしようか？

1311. It does not fit. Saizu ga aimasen.
サイズが合いません。

1312. Too [short] [long] [big] [small].
[Mijika] [Naga] [Ōki] [Chiisa] sugimasu.
[短か] [長] [大き] [小さ] 過ぎます。

1313. Can I order the same thing [in size 36]?
Kore no [sanjūroku no saizu] ga chūmon dekimasu ka?
これの［三十六のサイズ］が注文出来ますか？

1314. Please take the measurements.
Sumpō o totte kudasai. 寸法をとつて下さい。

1315. The length. Nagasa. 長さ。

1316. The width. Haba. 幅。

1317. The height. Takasa. 高さ。

1318. The depth. Fukasa. 深さ。

1319. Will it [shrink] [break]?
[Chijimu] [Kowareru] deshō ka?
［縮む］［壊れる］でしようか？

1320. Are these handmade? Tezukuri no mono deshō ka?
手作りの物でしようか？

1321. Is it [new]? [Atarashii mono] deshō ka?
［新しい物］でしようか？

1322. —secondhand. Furumono—. 古物一。

1323. —an antique. Kottōhin—. 骨董品一。

1324. —a replica. Mosha shita mono—.
模写した物一。

1325. —an imitation. Nisemono—. 贋物一。

1326. Is this colorfast? Iro no asenai mono desu ka?
色の褪せない物ですか？

1327. This is not my size.
Kore wa watakushi no saizu dewa arimasen.
これは私のサイズではありません。

1328. I like this one. Kore ga ki ni irimashita.
これが気に入リました。

1329. This will do. Kore de kekkō desu.
これで結構です。

1330. Please have this ready soon.
Isoide yōi shite oite kudasai.
急いで用意して置いて下さい。

1331. How long will it take to make the alterations?
Naosu no ni dono kurai nagaku kakarimasu ka?
直すのにどの位長くかゝりますか?

1332. Does the price include alterations?
Naoshidai mo haitte imasu ka?
直し代も入っいますか?

1333. I cannot decide. Kimeru koto ga dekimasen.
決めることが出来ません。

1334. I'll wait until it is ready.
Dekiagaru made matte imasu.
出来上がるまで待っています。

1335. Wrap this. Tsutsunde kudasai. 包んで下さい。

1336. Where do I pay? Doko de harau no desu ka?
どこで払うのですか?

1337. Do I pay [the salesman]?
[Sērusuman ni] harau no desu ka?
[セールス・マンに]払うのですか?

1338. —the salesgirl. Sērusugāru ni—. セールス・ガールに―。

1339. —the cashier. Reji (OR: Rejisutā) de—.
レジ（レジスター）で―。

1340. Will you honor this credit card?
Kono kurejitto kādo wa tsūyō shimasu ka?
このクレジット・カードは適用しますか？

1341. May I pay with a personal check?
Kogitte de haratte mo ii deshō ka?
小切手で払つてもいゝでしようか？

1342. Is this identification acceptable?
Kono mibun shōmeishō de ii deshō ka?
この身分証明証でいゝでしようか？

1343. Is the reference sufficient?
Kono shōmeishō de maniaimasu ka?
この証明証で間に合いますか？

1344. Can you send it to my hotel?
Hoteru made todokete moraemasu ka?
ホテルまで届けてもらえますか？

1345. Can you ship it to [New York City]?
[Nyū Yōku] made okutte moraemasu ka?
［ニュー・ヨーク］まで送つてもらえますか？

1346. Pack this for export.
Yushutsu no hōsō ni shite kudasai.
輸出の包装にして下さい。

1347. Give me [a bill]. [Kanjōgaki] o kudasai.
［勘定書］を下さい。

1348. —a receipt. Uketorishō—. 受取証 —。

1349. I shall pay upon delivery.
Uketori shidai haraimasu. 受取次第払います。

1350. Is there an additional charge for delivery?
Haitatsuryō wa betsu desu ka?
配達料は別ですか？

1351. I wish to return this article.
Kono shina o kaeshitai no desu ga.
この品を返えしたいのですが

1352. Refund my money.
Daikin o harai modoshite kudasai.
代金を払い戻して下さい。

1353. Please exchange this. Kore o torikaete kudasai.
これを取替えて下さい。

CLOTHING AND ACCESSORIES

1354. A cap. Kyappu. キャップ。

1355. A bathing cap. Kaisuibō. 海水帽。

1356. A bathing suit. Mizugi. 水着。

1357. A blouse. Burausu. ブラウス。

1358. An elastic belt. Gomu bando. ゴム・バンド。

1359. Boots. Būtsu. ブーツ。

1360. Bracelet. Buresuretto. ブレスレット。

1361. A brassiere. Burajā. ブラジャー。

1362. A button. Botan. ボタン。

1363. A cane. Sutekki. ステッキ。

1364. Japanese wooden clogs. Geta. 下駄。

1365. A coat. Kōto. コート。

1366. A collar. Karā. カラー。

1367. Cuffs. Kafusu. カフス。

1368. Cufflinks. Kafusu botan. カフス・ボタン。

1369. A dress. Doresu. ドレス。

1370. Children's dresses.
Kodomo no doresu (OR: Kodomo fuku).
子供のドレス（子供服）。

1371. Gloves. Tebukuro. 手袋。

1372. Handkerchief. Hankechi. ハンケチ。

1373. A hat. Bōshi. 帽子。

1374. A jacket. Uwagi. 上着。

1375. A dinner jacket. Takishīdo. タキシード。

1376. Jeans. Jīpan. ジーパン。

1377. Jewelry. Hōsekirui (OR: Akusessari).
宝石類（アクセッサリ）。

1378. A kimono. Kimono. 着物。

1379. A kimono coat. Haori. 羽織。

1380. A kimono sash. Obi. 帯。

1381. Kimono-skirt (for men). Hakama. 袴。

1382. Lingerie. Fujin-yō shitagirui. 婦人用下着類。

1383. A necktie. Nekutai. ネクタイ。

1384. A nightgown. Naitogaun (OR: Nemaki).
ナイト・ガウン（寝巻）。

1385. Pajamas. Pajama. パジャマ。

1386. Panties. Pantī. パンティー。

1387. A pin (decorative). Burōchi. ブローチ。

1388. A raincoat. Reinkōto. レイン・コート。

1389. Ribbon. Ribon. リボン。

1390. A ring. Ringu (OR: Yubiwa). リング（指環）。

1391. Rubbers. Gomugutsu (OR: Amagutsu).
ゴム靴（雨靴）。

1392. Sandals. Sandaru. サンダル。

1393. Japanese sandals. Zōri. 草履。

1394. A lady's scarf. Sukāfu. スカーフ。

1395. A man's scarf (OR: muffler). Mafurā. マフラー。

1396. A shawl. Shōru. ショール。

1397. A shirt. Waishatsu. ワイシャツ。

1398. Shoes. Kutsu. 靴。

1399. Shoelaces. Kutsu no himo. 靴の紐。

1400. Walking shorts (for men). Hanzubon. 半ズボン。

1401. A skirt. Sukāto. スカート。

1402. Slacks (for men). Surakkusu. スラックス。

1403. Slacks (for women). Pantaron. パンタロン。

1404. Sleeve. Sode. 袖。

1405. A slip. Surippu. スリップ。

1406. Slippers. Surippā. スリッパー。

1407. Socks (OR: Stockings). Sokkusu. ソックス。

1408. Straps (for Japanese sandals or clogs). Hanao. 鼻緒。

1409. A man's suit. Sebiro. 背広。

1410. A woman's suit. Sūtsu. スーツ。

1411. A sweater. Suētā. スエーター。

1412. A pair of trousers. Zubon. ズボン。

1413. Underwear. Shitagi. 下着。

1414. An umbrella. Yōgasa (OR: Kōmorigasa).
洋傘〔蝙蝠傘〕。

1415. Japanese umbrella. Bangasa (OR: Karakasa).
番傘（傘）。

1416. An undershirt. Shatsu. シャツ。

1417. Undershorts. Pantsu. パンツ。

COLORS

1418. Black. Kuro. 黒。

1419. Blue. Ao. 青。

1420. [Light] [Dark] brown. [Usu] [Koi] chairo.
〔薄〕〔濃い〕茶色。

1421. Cream. Kurīmu iro. クリーム色。

1422. Gray. Nezumi iro. 鼠色。

1423. Green. Midori iro. 緑色。

1424. Olive. Orību iro. オリーブ色。

1425. Orange. Orenji iro. オレンジ色。

1426. Pink. Pinku. ピンク。

1427. Purple. Murasaki. 紫。

1428. Red. Aka. 赤。

1429. White. Shiro. 白。

1430. Yellow. Kiiro. 黄色。

MATERIALS

1431. Metal. Kinzokurui. 金属類。

1432. Aluminum. Nyūmu (OR: Aruminyūmu). ニューム（アルミニューム）。

1433. Brass. Shinchū. 真鍮。

1434. Bronze. Seidō. 青銅。

1435. Copper. Dō (OR: Akagane). 銅。

1436. Iron. Tetsu. 鉄。

1437. Lead. Namari. 鉛。

1438. Gold. Kin. 金。

1439. Silver. Gin. 銀。

1440. Steel. Kōtetsu. 鋼鉄。

1441. Textiles. Orimonorui. 織物類。

1442. Cotton (fabric). Men orimono. 棉織物。

1443. Crêpe. Chirimen. 縮緬。

1444. Dacron. Dakuron. ダクロン。

1445. Flannel. Neru. ネル。

1446. Nylon. Nairon. ナイロン。

1447. Orlon. Oruron. オルロン。

1448. Rayon. Rēyon. レーヨン。

1449. Satin. Shusu. 繻子。

1450. Silk. Kinu. 絹。

1451. Synthetic. Gōsei no. 合成の。

1452. Wool. Ūru (OR: Keori). ウール（毛織）。

1453. Ceramics. Tōkirui. 陶器類。

1454. China. Setomono. 瀬戸物。

1455. Crystal. Kurisutaru. クリスタル。

1456. Fur. Kegawa. 毛皮。

1457. Glass. Garasu. ガラス。

1458. Lace. Rēsu. レース。

1459. Leather. Kawa. 皮（革）。

1460. Plastic. Purasuchikku (OR: Binīru).
プラスチック（ビニール）。

1461. Porcelain. Jiki seihin. 磁器製品。

55555

1462. Stone. Ishi. 石 。

1463. Wood. Ki. 木 。

BOOKSHOP, STATIONER AND NEWSDEALER

1464. Do you have any [books] in English?
Eigo no [hon] wa arimasu ka?
英語の[本]はありますか?

1465. Playing cards. Torampu. トランプ。

1466. A dictionary. Jisho. 辞書 。

1467. A dozen envelopes. Fūtō ichi dāsu.
封筒一ダース 。

1468. An eraser. Keshigomu. 消しゴム 。

1469. Fiction. Shōsetsu. 小説 。

1470. A guidebook. Annaisho. 案内書 。

1471. Ink. Inki. インキ 。

1472. A map. Chizu. 地図 。

1473. Magazines. Zasshi. 雑誌 。

1474. A newspaper. Shimbun. 新聞 。

1475. A notebook. Nōto (OR: Techō).
ノート (手帳) 。

1476. Airmail stationery. Kōkūbin-yō binsen.
航空便用便箋。

1477. Letter paper. Binsen. 便箋。

1478. Carbon paper. Kābon pēpā. カーボン・ペーパー。

1479. Onionskin paper. Fukusha yōshi. 複写用紙。

1480. Writing paper. Kakimono yōshi.
書き物用紙。

1481. Japanese writing paper. Hanshi. 半紙。

1482. Writing brush. Fude. 筆。

1483. A fountain pen. Mannenhitsu. 万年筆。

1484. A ballpoint pen. Bōru pen. ボール・ペン。

1485. A pencil. Empitsu. 鉛筆。

1486. An ever-sharp pencil. Shāpu penshiru.
シャープ・ペンシル。

1487. Postcards. Hagaki. 葉書。

1488. Picture postcards. Ehagaki. 絵葉書。

1489. Tape. Tēpu. テープ。

1490. Masking tape. Hogo tēpu. 保護テープ。

1491. Scotch tape. Sero tēpu. セロ・テープ。

1492. Stapler. Hotchikisu. ホッチキス。

1493. String. Himo. 紐。

1494. A typewriter. Taipuraitā. タイプライター。

1495. Typewriter ribbon. Taipuraitāyō ribon.
タイプライター用リボン。

1496. Wrapping paper. Tsutsumigami. 包み紙。

PHARMACY

1497. Is there [a pharmacy] here where they understand English?
Koko ni eigo no tsūjiru [kusuriya] wa arimasu ka?
こゝに英語の通じる[薬屋]はありますか?

1498. May I speak to [a male clerk]?
[Otoko no ten-in] ni hanashitai no desu ga.
[男の店員]に話したいのですが。

1499. —a female clerk. Onna no ten-in—.
女の店員一。

1500. Can you fill this prescription [immediately]?
Kono shohō no chōzai wa [sugu] dekimasu ka?
この処方の調剤は[直ぐ]出来ますか?

1501. Is it mild? Shigekisei no sukunai mono deshō ka?
刺戟性の少ない物でしようか?

1502. Is it safe? Anzen deshō ka? 安全でしようか?

1503. Antibiotic. Kōsei busshitsu. 抗生物質。

1504. Pain-killer. Chintsūzai. 鎮痛剤。

1505. Sleeping pill. Suiminzai. 睡眠剤.

1506. Tranquilizer (OR: **Sedative**). Chinseizai. 鎮静剤.

1507. Caution. Chūi. 注意.

1508. Poison. Dokuyaku. 毒薬.

1509. Take as directed. Shijidōri fukuyō no koto.
指示通り服用のこと.

1510. For external use only. Gaiyōyaku. 外用薬.

DRUGSTORE ITEMS

1511. Adhesive tape. Bansōkō. 絆創膏.

1512. Analgesic (OR: **Aspirin**). Chintsūzai (OR: Asupirin).
鎮痛剤 (アスピリン).

1513. Alcohol. Arukōru. アルコール.

1514. Antiseptic. Shōdokueki. 消毒液.

1515. Band-Aids. Bando ēdo. バンド・エード.

1516. Bandages. Hōtai. 繃帯.

1517. Bicarbonate of soda. Jūtansan sōda.
重炭酸曹達.

1518. Bobby pins. Bobi pin. ボビ・ピン.

1519. Boric acid. Hōsan. 硼酸.

1520. Chewing gum. Chūingamu. チュイン ガム 。

1521. Cleaning fluid. Kurīninguyō kihatsuyu.
クリーニング用揮発油 。

1522. Cleansing tissues. Tisshu pēpā. ティッシュ・ペーパー。

1523. Cold cream. Korudo kurīmu. コルド・クリーム 。

1524. Cologne. Koronsui. コロン水 。

1525. Comb. Kushi. 櫛 。

1526. Compact. Kompakuto. コンパクト 。

1527. Contraceptives (for men). Kondōmu. コンドーム 。

1528. Contraceptives (for women). Hinin yōgu.
避姙用具 。

1529. Corn pad. Mame ni haru kōyaku.
まめに貼る膏薬 。

1530. Cotton (absorbent). Dasshimen. 脱脂綿 。

1531. Cough syrup. Sekidome. 咳止め 。

1532. Deodorant. Bōshūzai. 防臭剤 。

1533. Depilatory. Datsumōzai. 脱毛剤 。

1534. Disinfectant. Shōdokuyaku. 消毒薬 。

1535. Earplugs. Mimi sen. 耳栓 。

1536. Epsom salts. Shari-en. 舎利塩 。

1537. Eye cup. Sengan-yō koppu. 洗眼用コップ。

1538. Eye wash. Sengan-yaku. 洗眼薬 。

1539. Gauze. Gāze. ガーゼ 。

1540. Hairbrush. Heyā burashi. ヘヤー・ブラシ。

1541. Hair clip. Heyā kurippu. ヘヤー・クリップ。

1542. Hair net. Heyā netto. ヘヤー・ネット。

1543. Hair·pins. Heyā pin. ヘヤー・ピン。

1544. Hair spray. Heyā supurē. ヘヤー・スプレー。

1545. Hair tonic. Heyā tonikku. ヘヤー・トニック。

1546. Hand lotion. Rōshon. ローション。

1547. Hot-water bottle. Yutampo. 湯湯婆 。

1548. Ice bag. Hyōnō. 氷嚢 。

1549. Insecticide. Bōchūzai. 防虫剤 。

1550. Iodine. Yōdo. ヨード。

1551. Laxative (mild). Gezai (karui). 下剤 (軽い)。

1552. Lipstick. Kuchibeni (OR: Rūju). 口紅 (ルージュ)。

1553. Medicine dropper. Tentekiki. 点滴器 。

1554. Mouthwash. Kuchiyusugi. 口漱ぎ。

1555. Nail file. Tsume no yasuri. 爪のやすり。

1556. Nail polish. Tsume migaki. 爪磨き。

1557. Nose drops. Hana no tentekiyaku. 鼻の点滴薬。

1558. Ointment. Nankō. 軟膏。

1559. Peroxide. Kasanka suiso. 過酸化水素。

1560. Pin. Pin. ピン。

1561. Powdered medicine. San-yaku. 散薬。

1562. Face powder. Oshiroi. 白粉。

1563. Foot powder. Ashi no tame no paudā. 足の為のパウダー。

1564. Talcum powder. Taruku. タルク。

1565. Powder puff. Pafu. パフ。

1566. Straight razor. Kamisori. 剃刀。

1567. Electric razor. Denki kamisori. 電気剃刀。

1568. Safety razor. Anzen kamisori. 安全剃刀。

1569. Razor blade. Kamisori no ha. 剃刀の刃。

1570. Rouge. Hōbeni (OR: Rūju). 頬紅（ルージュ）。

1571. Safety pin. Anzen pin. 安全ピン。

1572. Sanitary napkins. Seiritai (OR: Tampakusu).
生理帯（タンパクス）.

1573. Scissors. Hasami. 鋏.

1574. Shampoo. Shampū. シャンプー.

1575. Shaving brush. Higesoriyō burashi.
髭剃リ用ブラシ.

1576. Shaving cream. Higesoriyō kurīmu.
髭剃リ用クリーム.

1577. Shaving lotion. Higesoriyō rōshon.
髭剃リ用ローション.

1578. Shower cap. Shawāyō kyappu. シャワー用キャップ.

1579. Smelling salts. Kagigusuri (OR: Kitsukegusuri).
嗅薬（気付薬）.

1580. Soap. Sekken. 石けん.

1581. Sponge. Suponji. スポンジ.

1582. Sunburn ointment. Hiyakeyō tannankō.
日焼け用単軟膏.

1583. Sunglasses. Sangurasu. サン・グラス.

1584. Suntan oil. Santan oiru. サンタン・オイル.

1585. Syringe. Senjōki (OR: Supoito).
洗浄器（スポイト）.

1586. Thermometer [Celsius] [Fahrenheit].
Taionkei [sesshi] [kashi].
体温計 [摂氏][華氏]。

1587. Toothbrush.   Ha burashi.   歯ブラシ。

1588. Toothpaste.   Neri hamigaki.   練り歯磨。

1589. Toothpowder.   Hamigaki ko. 歯磨き粉。

1590. Vaseline.   Waserin.   ワセリン。

1591. Vitamins.   Bitamin.   ビタミン。

CAMERA SHOP AND PHOTOGRAPHY

1592. I want a roll of film [for this camera].
[Kono kamera no] firumu ga hoshii no desu ga.
[このカメラの] フィルムが欲しいのですが。

1593. Do you have [color film]?
[Karā firumu] wa arimasu ka?
[カラー・フィルム] はありますか？

1594. —black-and-white film.   Kuro shiro no firumu—.
黒白の フィルム—。

1595. —16 mm film.   Jūroku miri no firumu—.
十六ミリの フィルム—。

1596. —35 mm film.   Sanjūgo miri no firumu—.
三十五ミリの フィルム—。

1597. What is the charge [for developing a roll]?
[Genzō wa ikko] ikura desu ka?
[現像は一箇] いくらでずか?

1598. —for enlarging. Hikinobashi wa—.
引伸ばしは一。

1599. —for one print. Purinto ichimai wa—.
プリント一枚は一。

1600. May I take a [photo] of you?
Anata no [shashin] o totte mo ii deshō ka?
あなたの[写真]をとってもいいでしょうか?

1601. Would you take a photo of me, please?
Watakushi no shashin o totte kudasaimasen ka?
私の写真をとって下さいませんか?

1602. A color print. Karā purinto. カラー・プリント。

1603. Flashbulbs. Furasshu rampu. フラッシュ・ランプ。

1604. The lens. Renzu. レンズ。

1605. The negative. Nega. ネガ。

1606. The shutter. Shattā. シメッター。

1607. A transparency. Suraido. スライド。

1608. A tripod. Sankyaku. 三脚。

GIFT AND SOUVENIR LIST

1609. Basket.   Basuketto.   バスケット。

1610. Batik.   Rōketsuzome.   ろうけつ染め。

1611. Box of chocolates.   Hakozume chokorēto.
箱詰めのチョコレート。

1612. Brocade (OR: *Obi* **material**).   Nishiki (OR: Obiji).
錦(帯地)。

1613. Cloisonné.   Shippōyaki.   七宝焼。

1614. Doll.   Ningyō.   人形。

1615. Earrings.   Iya ringu.   イヤ・リング。

1616. Embroidery.   Shishū.   刺しゆう。

1617. Handicrafts.   Shugeihin.   手芸品。

1618. Incense.   Okō.   お香。

1619. Incense burners.   Kōro.   香炉。

1620. Ivory pendants.   Netsuke (OR: Zōge no netsuke).
根付け(象牙の根付け)。

1621. Jade.   Hisui.   翡翠。

1622. Jewelry.   Hōsekirui.   宝石類。

1623. Lacquerware.   Urushi no nurimono.
漆の塗物。

1624. Painted screens. Byōbu. 屏風。

1625. Pearls. Shinju. 真珠。

1626. Perfume. Kōsui. 香水。

1627. Phonograph records. Rekōdo. レコード。

1628. Pottery. Tōjiki rui. 陶磁器類。

1629. Woodblock prints. Mokuhanga (OR: Hanga).
木版画（版画）。

1630. A radio. Rajio. ラジオ。

1631. Reproduction (of painting, etc.). Fukusei. 複製。

1632. Silk materials. Kinuji. 絹地。

1633. Souvenir. Miyagemono (OR: Sūbeniru).
土産物（スーベニル）。

1634. Tape recorder. Tēpu rokuonki. テープ録音機。

1635. Toys. Omocha. 玩具。

1636. Transistor radio. Toranjisutā. トランジスター。

1637. Wrist watch. Udedokei. 腕時計。

TOBACCO STORE

1638. Where is the [nearest] tobacco store?
[Ichiban chikai] tabakoya wa doko deshō ka?
［一番近い］タバコ屋はどこでしようか？

1639. I want some [cigars].   [Hamaki] ga hoshii no desu ga.
[葉巻] が欲しいのですが。

1640. What brands of American cigarettes do you have?
Amerika-sei no tabako de wa donna no ga arimasu ka?
アメリカ製のタバコではどんなのがありますか？

1641. What brands do you have with menthol?
Mensoru (OR: Hakka) tabako de wa donna no ga arimasu
　ka?
メンソル（はっか、）タバコではどんなのがありますか？

1642. One pack of king-size filter-tip cigarettes.
Kingu saizu firutā-tsuki tabako o ikko.
キング・サイズ フィルター付きタバコを一箇。

1643. I need a lighter.   Raitā ga hoshii no desu ga.
ライターが欲しいのですが。

1644. Lighter fluid.   Raitā oiru. ライター・オイル。

1645. Flint.   Raitā no ishi. ライターの石。

1646. Matches.   Matchi. マッチ。

1647. A pipe.   Paipu. パイプ。

1648. A Japanese-style pipe.   Kiseru. キセル。

1649. Pipe cleaners.   Paipu kurīnā. パイプ・クリーナー。

1650. Pipe tobacco.   Paipu tabako (OR: Kizami tabako).
パイプ・タバコ（刻みタバコ）。

1651. A tobacco pouch.   Paipu tabako ire.
パイプ・タバコ入れ。

LAUNDRY AND DRY CLEANING

1652. Where is [the laundry]?
[Sentakuya] wa doko deshō ka?
[洗濯屋] は どこ でしようか？

1653. Is there a dry-cleaning service near here?
Dorai kurīninguya wa chikaku ni arimasu ka?
ドライ・クリーニング屋 は 近く に ありますか？

1654. Wash this blouse in [hot water].
Kono burausu wa [netsuyu] de aratte kudasai.
この ブラウス は [熱湯] で 洗つて下さい。

1655. —warm water. —yu. 一湯。

1656. —lukewarm water. —nurumayu. 一ぬるま湯。

1657. —cold water. —mizu. 一水。

1658. No starch, please. Nori o tsukenai de kudasai.
糊 を 付けないで下さい。

1659. Remove this stain from [this shirt].
[Kono shatsu] no shimi o nuite kudasai.
[この シヤツ] の 染み を 抜いて下さい。

1660. Press [the trousers].
[Zubon] o puresu shite kudasai.
[ズボン] を プレス して下さい。

1661. Starch [the collar].
[Karā] ni nori o tsukete kudasai.
[カラー] に 糊 を 付けて下さい。

1662. Dry-clean [this coat].
[Kono kōto] o dorai kurīningu shite kudasai.
[このコート] を ドライ・クリーニング して下さい。

1663. [The belt] is missing.
[Bando (OR: Beruto)] ga arimasen.
[バンド (ベルト)] が ありません。

1664. Sew on [this button].
[Kono botan] o tsukete kudasai.
[このボタン] を 付けて下さい。

REPAIRS AND ADJUSTMENTS

1665. This watch [is fast] [is slow].
Kono tokei wa [susunde] [okurete] imasu.
この 時計 は [進んで] [遅れて] います。

1666. [My glasses] are broken.
[Megane] ga kowaremashita. [眼鏡] が 毀れました。

1667. It is torn.   Yaburete imasu. 破れています。

1668. Where can I get it repaired?
Doko de naoshite moraemasu ka?
どこで 直してもらえますか?

1669. Please fix [this lock].
[Kono jō] o naoshite kudasai.
[この 錠] を 直して下さい。

1670. Fix [the sole] [the heel].
Kono [kutsu no soko] [kakato] o shūrishite kudasai.
この [靴の底] [かゝと] を 修理して下さい。

1671. Adjust this [hearing aid].
Kono [hochōki] o chōsetsu shite kudasai.
この[補聴器]を調節して下さい。

1672. Lengthen [this skirt].
[Kono sukāto] o nagaku shite kudasai.
[このスカート]を長くして下さい。

1673. Shorten [the sleeves].
[Sode] o mijikaku shite kudasai.
[袖]を短かくして下さい。

1674. Replace [the lining].   [Uraji] o kaete kudasai.
[裏地]を替えて下さい。

1675. Mend [the pocket].   [Poketto] o tsukurotte kudasai.
[ポケット]を繕って下さい。

1676. Clean [the mechanism].
[Kikai sōchi] o kirei ni shite kudasai.
[機械装置]をきれいにして下さい。

1677. Lubricate [the spring].
[Supuringu] ni abura o sashite kudasai.
[スプリング]に油を差して下さい。

1678. Needle.   Nuibari. 縫針。

1679. Thimble.   Yubinuki. 指貫き。

1680. Thread.   Nui-ito. 縫い糸。

BARBER SHOP

1681. Where is there [a barber shop]?
[Rihatsuten] wa doko deshō ka?
［理髪店］はどこでしようか？

1682. A haircut, please.   Sampatsu negaimasu.
散髪願います。

1683. A light trim.   Karuku tsunde kudasai.
軽く剪んで下さい。

1684. I want a shave.   Hige o sotte kudasai.
髭を剃つて下さい。

1685. Please give me a shoeshine.
Kutsu o migaite kudasai. 靴を磨いて下さい。

1686. Don't cut much [off the top] [on the sides].
[Ue no hō] [Yoko no hō] wa amari karanaide kudasai.
［上の方］［横の方］は余り刈らないで下さい。

1687. I want to keep my hair long.
Kami wa nagakushite okitai no desu.
髪は長くして置きたいのです。

1688. I part my hair [on this side].
[Kochiragawa de] wakemasu. ［こちら側で］分けます。

1689. —on the other side.   Hantaigawa de—.
反対側で—。

1690. —in the middle.   Mannaka de—. 真中で—。

1691. No hair tonic.   Heyā tonikku wa tsukenaide.
ヘヤー・トニックは付けないで。

1692. Trim my [mustache] [beard].
[Kuchihige] [Agohige] o sukoshi katte kudasai.
[口髭][あご髭]を少し刈つて下さい。

1693. Scissors only, please.　Hasami dake ni shite kudasai.
鋏だけにして下さい。

BEAUTY PARLOR

1694. Can I make an appointment for [Monday afternoon]?
[Getsuyō no gogo] ni onegai dekimasu ka?
[月曜の午後]にお願い出来ますか?

1695. Comb my hair.　Kami o toite kudasai.
髪を解いて下さい。

1696. Wash my hair.　Atama o aratte kudasai.
頭を洗つて下さい。

1697. Shampoo and set, please.
Shampū to setto o shite kudasai.
シャンプーとセットをして下さい。

1698. Not too short.　Amari mijikaku shinaide.
余り短かくしないで。

1699. In this style, please.　Kono sutairu ni shite kudasai.
このスタイルにして下さい。

1700. Dye my hair [in this shade].
[Kono iro ni] somete kudasai.
[この色に]染めて下さい。

1701. Clean and set this wig.
Kono wigu o kirei ni shite setto shite kudasai.
このウィグをきれいにしてセットして下さい。

1702. A curl. Kāru. カール。

1703. A beauty treatment. Gammen massāji.
顔面マッサージ。

1704. A hairpiece. Heyā pīsu. ヘヤー・ピース。

1705. Hair rinse. Heyā rinsu. ヘヤー・リンス。

1706. A massage. Massāji. マッサージ。

1707. A manicure. Manikyua. マニキュア。

1708. A permanent wave. Pāma (OR: Pāmanento).
パーマ（パーマネント）。

STORES AND SERVICES

1709. Antique shop. Kottōya. 骨董屋。

1710. Art gallery. Garō. 画廊。

1711. Artist's materials. Ekakiyō dōgu. 絵書き用道具。

1712. Auto rental. Rentakā. レンタ・カー。

1713. Auto repairs. Jidōsha shūriya. 自動車修理屋。

1714. Bakery. Bēkarī (OR: Pan-ya). ベーカリー（パン屋）。

1715. Bank. Ginkō. 銀行。

1716. Bar. Bā. バー。

1717. Barber. Rihatsuten. 理髪店。

1718. Beauty salon. Biyōin. 美容院。

1719. Bookshop. Hon-ya. 本屋。

1720. Butcher. Nikuya. 肉屋。

1721. Candy shop. Kyandēya. キャンデー屋。

1722. Checkroom. (Keitaihin) azukarijo.
（携帯品）預かり所。

1723. Clothing store (Western). Yōfukuya. 洋服屋。

1724. Clothing store (Japanese). Gofukuten. 呉服店。

1725. Cosmetics shop. Keshōhinten. 化粧品店。

1726. Dance studio. Dansu sutajio. ダンス・スタジオ。

1727. Dentist. Ha-isha. 歯医者。

1728. Department store. Depāto. デパート。

1729. Dressmaker. Doresu mēkā. ドレス・メーカー。

1730. Drugstore. Kusuriya. 薬屋。

1731. Electrical supplies. Denki yōhin. 電気用品。

1732. Employment agency. Shokugyō shōkaijo.
職業紹介所。

1733. Fancy goods store. Yōhinten. 洋品店。

1734. Fish store. Sakanaya. 魚屋。

1735. **Florist.**   Hanaya. 花屋 。

1736. **Fruit store.**   Kudamonoya. 果物屋 。

1737. **Furniture store.**   Kaguya. 家具屋 。

1738. **Grocery.**   Shokuryōhinten. 食料品店 。

1739. **Ladies' hairdresser.**   Biyōin. 美容院 。

1740. **Men's hairdresser.**   Rihatsuten (OR: Sampatsuya).
理髪店 (散髪屋)。

1741. **Hardware store.**   Kanamonoya. 金物屋 。

1742. **Hat shop.**   Bōshiya. 帽子屋 。

1743. **Housewares.**   Zakkaten. 雑貨店 。

1744. **Jewelry store.**   Hōsekiya. 宝石屋 。

1745. **Lawyer.**   Bengoshi. 弁護士 。

1746. **Laundry.**   Sentakuya. 洗濯屋 。

1747. **Liquor store.**   Sakaya. 酒屋 。

1748. **Loan office.**   Kashitsukejo. 箕付所 。

1749. **Lumber dealer.**   Zaimokuya. 材木屋 。

1750. **Market.**   Māketto. マーケット 。

1751. **Milliner.**   Fujin bōshiya. 婦人帽子屋 。

1752. **Money exchange.**   Ryōgaeya. 両替屋 。

1753. Music store. Gakkiten. 楽器店。

1754. Musical instruments. Gakki. 楽器。

1755. Newsstand. Shimbun baiten. 新聞売店。

1756. Sheet music. Gakufu. 楽譜。

1757. Paints (for artists). Enogu. 絵具。

1758. Paints (for household use). Penki. ペンキ。

1759. Pastry shop. Yōgashiya. 洋菓子屋。

1760. Photographer. Shashin-ya. 写真屋。

1761. Post office. Yūbinkyoku. 郵便局。

1762. Printing shop. Insatsujo. 印刷所。

1763. Public baths. Sentō (OR: Furoya). 銭湯(風呂屋)。

1764. Sewing machines. Mishin. ミシン。

1765. Shoemaker. Kutsunaoshi. 靴直し。

1766. Shoe store. Kutsuya. 靴屋。

1767. Sightseeing. Kankō (OR: Kembutsu). 観光(見物)。

1768. Sign painter. Kamban-ya. 看板屋。

1769. Sporting goods. Undōguya. 運動具屋。

1770. Stockbroker. Kabushiki nakagainin.
株式仲買人。

1771. Supermarket. Sūpāmāketto. スーパー・マーケット。

1772. Tailor. Tērā (OR: Shitateya). テーラー (仕立屋)。

1773. Toy shop. Omochaya. 玩具屋。

1774. Trucking. Torakku unsō. トラック運送。

1775. Used cars. Chūkosha. 中古車。

1776. Vegetable store. Yaoya. 八百屋。

1777. Watchmaker. Tokeiya. 時計屋。

BABY CARE

1778. I need a reliable babysitter tonight [at 7 o'clock].
Komban [shichiji ni] shin-yō dekiru komori ga irimasu ga.
今晩 [七時に] 信用出来る子守がいりますが。

1779. Call a pediatrician immediately.
Shōnika-i o sugu yonde kudasai.
小児科医を直ぐ呼んで下さい。

1780. Sterilize the bottle.
Gyūnyūki o shōdoku shite kudasai.
牛乳器を消毒し下さい。

1781. Change the diaper. Oshime o kaete kudasai.
おしめを替えて下さい。

1782. Bathe the baby. Kodomo o furo ni irete kudasai.
子供を風呂に入れて下さい。

1783. Put the baby in the crib for a nap.
Hirune wa kodomo no beddo de.
昼寝は子供のベッドで。

1784. Give the baby a pacifier when he cries.
Nakimashitara oshaburi o yatte kudasai.
泣きましたらおしゃぶりをやって下さい。

1785. Do you have an ointment for diaper rash?
Oshime no kaburedome wa arimasu ka?
おしめのかぶれ止めはありますか?

1786. Take the baby to the park in the carriage (OR: **stroller**).
Ubaguruma de kōen e tsurete itte kudasai.
乳母車で公園へ連れて行って下さい。

1787. Baby food.   Nyūji eiyōshoku. 乳児栄養食。

1788. Baby powder.   Bebīyō paudā. ベビー用パウダー。

1789. Bib.   Yodarekake. よだれ掛け。

1790. Colic.   Fukutsū. 腹痛。

1791. High chair.   Bebīyō isu. ベビー用いす。

1792. Nursemaid.   Uba (OR: **Komori**). 乳母(子守)。

1793. Playground.   Yūenchi. 遊園地。

1794. Rattle.   Garagara. ガラガラ。

HEALTH AND ILLNESS

1795. Is the doctor [at home] [at the hospital]?
Isha wa [otaku] [byōin] desu ka?
医者 は［お宅］［病院］ですか？

1796. What are his office hours?
Shinsatsu jikan wa itsu desu ka?
診察時間 はいつですか？

1797. Take my temperature. Netsu o hakatte kudasai.
熱を計って下さい。

1798. I have something [in my eye].
[Me ni] nanika hairimashita. ［目に］何か入りました。

1799. I have a pain in [my back]. [Senaka] ga itamimasu.
［背中］が痛みます。

1800. My [toe] is swollen. [Ashi no yubi] ga harete imasu.
［足の指］がはれています。

1801. It is sensitive to pressure. Osaeru to itamimasu.
押えると痛みます。

1802. Is it [a serious illness]? [Jūbyō] desu ka?
［重病］ですか？

1803. I do not sleep well. Yoku nemuremasen.
よく眠れません。

1804. I have no appetite. Shokuyoku ga arimasen.
食欲がありません。

1805. Can you give me something to relieve the pain?
Itamidome ni nanika itadakemashō ka?
痛み止めに何か頂けましょうか？

1806. Where should I have [this prescription] filled?
[Kono shohō] wa doko de chōzaishite moraemasu ka?
［この処方］はどこで調剤してもらえますか？

1807. Do I have to go to [a hospital]?
[Byōin] ni ikanakereba naranai deshō ka?
［病院］に行かなければならないでしょうか？

1808. Is surgery required?   Shujutsu o yōshimasu ka?
手術を要しますか？

1809. Must I stay in bed?   Nete inakereba narimasen ka?
寝ていなければなりませんか？

1810. When will I begin to feel better?
Itsugoro kara yoku narimashō ka?
いつ頃からよくなりましようか？

1811. Is it contagious?   Densen shimasu ka?
伝染しますか？

1812. I feel [better] [worse].
[Ikuraka yoku] [Waruku] narimashita.
［いくらかよく］［悪く］なりました。

1813. There has been no change.   Kawari arimasen.
変りありません。

1814. Shall I keep it bandaged?
Hōtai no mama ni shite oku no desu ka?
包帯のまゝにして置くのですか？

1815. Can I travel [on Monday]?
[Getsuyōbi ni] ryokō ga dekimashō ka?
［月曜日に］旅行が出来ましようか？

1816. When will you come again?
Itsu mata kite kudasaimasu ka?
いつ又来て下さいますか?

1817. When should I take [the medicine] [the pills]?
[Kusuri] [Gan-yaku] wa itsu nomu no desu ka?
[薬] [丸薬] はいつ飲むのですか?

1818. When do I get the injections?
Chūsha wa itsu suru no desu ka?
注射はいつするのですか?

1819. Every hour. Ichijikan goto. 一時間毎。

1820. [Before] [after] meals. Shoku [zen] [go].
食 [前] [後] 。

1821. On going to bed. Neru mae. 寝る前。

1822. On getting up. Oki shidai. 起き次第。

1823. Twice a day. Hi ni nikai. 日に二回。

1824. An anesthetic. Masuizai. 麻酔剤。

1825. Convalescence. Kaifukuki. 回復期。

1826. Cure. Chiryō. 治療。

1827. Diet. Kiteishoku. 規定食。

1828. Eye drops (OR: **Eye wash**). Megusuri. 目薬。

1829. Nurse. Kangofu. 看護婦。

1830. An orthopedist. Seikeigeka-i. 整形外科医。

1831. An oculist. Ganka-i. 眼科医

1832. Remedy. Chiryōhō. 治療法。

1833. A specialist. Semmon-i. 専門医。

1834. A surgeon. Geka-i. 外科医。

1835. A teaspoonful. Kosaji ippai. 小さじ一杯。

1836. Treatment. Chiryō. 治療。

1837. X-ray. Rentogen. レントゲン。

AILMENTS

1838. An allergy. Arerugī. アレルギー。

1839. Appendicitis. Mōchōen. 盲腸炎。

1840. I have been bitten by an insect.
Mushi ni sasaremashita. 虫にさゝれました。

1841. A blister. Mizubukure. 水ぶくれ。

1842. A bruise. Uchimi. 打身。

1843. A burn. Yakedo. 火傷。

1844. Chicken pox. Mizubōsō. 水疱瘡。

1845. A chill. Samuke. 寒気。

1846. A cold. Kaze. 風邪。

1847. A corn. Mame. まめ。

1848. A cut. Kirikizu. 切り傷。

1849. Constipation. Bempi. 便秘。

1850. A cough. Seki. 咳。

1851. A [muscle] cramp. [Kinniku no] keiren.
[筋肉の] けいれん。

1852. Diarrhea. Geri. 下痢。

1853. Dysentery. Sekiri. 赤痢。

1854. An earache. Mimi no itami. 耳の痛み。

1855. An epidemic. Ryūkōbyō. 流行病。

1856. To feel faint. Furafura suru. フラフラする。

1857. A fever. Hatsunetsu (OR: Netsu).
発熱 (熱)。

1858. Hay fever. Kafunshō. 花粉症。

1859. A fracture. Kossetsu. 骨折。

1860. Headache. Zutsū. 頭痛。

1861. Indigestion. Fushōka. 不消化。

1862. Infection. Kansen. 感染。

1863. Inflammation. Enshō. 炎症。

1864. Influenza. Infuruenza. インフルエンザ。

1865. Insomnia. Fuminshō. 不眠症。

1866. Measles. Hashika. はしか。

1867. Mumps. Otafukukaze. お多福風。

1868. Nausea. Hakike. 吐き気。

1869. Nosebleed. Hanaji. 鼻血。

1870. Pneumonia. Haien. 肺炎。

1871. Poisoning. Chūdoku. 中毒。

1872. A sprain. Sujichigai. 筋違い。

1873. A sore throat. Nodo no itami. 喉の痛み。

1874. I have been stung by a bee. Hachi ni sasaremashita. 蜂にさゝれました。

1875. A sunburn. Hiyake. 日焼け。

1876. A swelling (OR: **boil**). Haremono. はれ物。

1877. Tonsillitis. Hentōsen-en. 扁桃腺炎。

1878. Toothache. Ha no itami. 歯の痛み。

1879. To vomit. Modosu (OR: Haku). 戻す(吐く)。

DENTIST

1880. Can you recommend [a good dentist]?
[Yoi ha-isha] o shōkai shite itadakemashō ka?
[よい歯医者]を紹介して頂けましょうか？

1881. I have lost a filling. Tsumemono ga toremashita.
詰物がとれました。

1882. Can you replace the filling?
Tsume-naosemasu ka? 詰め直せますか？

1883. Can you fix [the bridge] [this denture]?
[Burijji] [Kono ireba] wa naosemasu ka?
［ブリッジ］［この入れ歯］は直せますか？

1884. This [tooth] hurts me. Kono [ha] ga itamimasu.
この［歯］が痛みます。

1885. My gums are sore. Haguki ga itamimasu.
歯ぐきが痛みます。

1886. My tooth is broken. Ha ga oremashita.
歯が折れました。

1887. I have [an abscess]. [Nōyō] desu.
［膿瘍］です。

1888. —a cavity. Mushiba—. 虫歯—。

1889. Please give me [a general anesthetic].
[Zenshin masui] ni shite kudasai.
［全身麻酔］にして下さい。

1890. —a local anesthetic. Kyokubu masui—.
局部麻酔—。

1891. —a temporary filling. Kari no tsumemono—.
仮の詰物—。

1892. I do not want the tooth extracted.
Nukitakunai no desu ga.
抜きたくないのですが。

ACCIDENTS

1893. There has been an accident. Jiko ga arimashita.
事故がありました。

1894. Get [a doctor] immediately.
[Isha] o sugu yonde kudasai. [医者]を直ぐ呼んで下さい。

1895. —an ambulance. Kyūkyūsha—. 救急車—。

1896. —a policeman. Keikan (OR: Porisu)—.
警官（ポリス）—。

1897. He has collapsed. Taoremashita. 倒れました。

1898. She has fainted. Sottō shimashita. 卒倒しました。

1899. He is injured. Kega o shimashita.
怪我をしました。

1900. Do not move [her] [him]. Ugokasanaide kudasai.
動かさないで下さい。

1901. [My finger] is bleeding.
[Yubi] ga shukketsushite imasu.
[指]が出血しています。

1902. A fracture [of the arm]. [Ude no] kossetsu.
[腕の]骨折。

1903. Notify [my husband] [my wife].
[Shujin] [Kanai] ni shirasete kudasai.
[主人][家内]に知らせて下さい。

1904. A tourniquet. Shiketsutai. 止血帯。

1905. I want to rest.   Yasumitai no desu.
休みたいのです。

1906. I want to sit down.   Suwaritai no desu.
座りたいのです。

1907. I want to lie down.   Yoko ni naritai no desu.
横になりたいのです。

PARTS OF THE BODY

1908. Ankle.   Ashikubi.   足首。

1909. Appendix.   Mōchō.   盲腸。

1910. Arm.   Ude.   腕。

1911. Armpit.   Waki no shita.   脇の下。

1912. Artery.   Dōmyaku.   動脈。

1913. Back.   Senaka.   背中。

1914. Belly.   Onaka (OR: Hara; OR: Fukubu).
お中（腹；腹部）。

1915. Blood.   Chi.   血。

1916. Blood vessel.   Kekkan.   血管。

1917. Body.   Karada.   体。

1918. Bone.   Hone.   骨。

1919. Brain.   Nō.   脳。

1920. Breast. Chibusa. 乳房。

1921. Calf. Fukurahagi. 脹うはぎ。

1922. Cheek. Hō. ほか(頬)。

1923. Chest. Mune. 胸。

1924. Chin. Ago. あご。

1925. Collarbone. Sakotsu. 鎖骨。

1926. Ear. Mimi. 耳。

1927. Elbow. Hiji. 肘。

1928. Eye. Me. 目(眼)。

1929. Eyebrow. Mayu. 眉。

1930. Eyelashes. Matsuge. まつげ。

1931. Eyelid. Mabuta. 瞼。

1932. Face. Kao. 顔。

1933. Finger. Yubi. 指。

1934. Fingernail. Te no tsume. 手の爪。

1935. Foot. Ashi. 足。

1936. Forehead. Hitai. 額。

1937. Gall bladder. Tannō. 胆のう。

1938. Genitals. Seishokki. 性殖器.

1939. Glands. Sen. 腺.

1940. Hair. Kami no ke (OR: Ke). 髪の毛 (毛).

1941. Hand. Te. 手.

1942. Head. Atama. 頭.

1943. Heart. Shinzō. 心臓.

1944. Heel. Kakato. かゝと.

1945. Hip. Koshi. 腰.

1946. Intestines. Chō. 腸.

1947. Jaw. Ago. あご.

1948. Joint. Kansetsu. 関節.

1949. Kidney. Jinzō. じん臓.

1950. Knee. Hiza. ひざ.

1951. Larynx. Kōtō. こう頭. 喉頭

1952. Leg. Ashi. 足.

1953. Lip. Kuchibiru. くちびる.

1954. Liver. Kanzō. 肝臓.

1955. Lungs. Hai. 肺.

1956. Mouth. Kuchi. 口。

1957. Muscle. Kinniku. 筋肉。

肚臍 **1958. Navel.** Heso. へそ。

1959. Neck. Kubi. 首。

1960. Nerve. Shinkei. 神経。

1961. Nose. Hana. 鼻。

1962. Palm. Tenohira. 手の平。

1963. Pancreas. Suizō. すい臓。

1964. Rib. Rokkotsu. 肋骨。

1965. Shin. Sune. すね。

1966. Shoulder. Kata. 肩。

1967. Side. Yokoppara. 横っ腹。

1968. Skin. Hifu. 皮膚。

1969. Skull. Tōgai. 頭蓋。

1970. Spine. Sekizui. せき骨髄。

1971. Spleen. Hizō. 脾臓。

1972. Stomach. I. 胃。

1973. Temple. Komekami. こめかみ。

1974. Thigh.   Futomomo. 太股.

1975. Throat.   Nodo. のど.

1976. Thumb.   Oyayubi. 親指.

1977. Toe.   Tsumasaki. 爪先.

1978. Tongue.   Shita. 舌.

1979. Tonsils.   Hentōsen. へんとうせん.

1980. Waist.   Hosogoshi. 細腰.

1981. Wrist.   Tekubi. 手首.

TIME

1982. What time is it?   Nanji desu ka? 何時ですか?

1983. Two A.M.   Gozen niji. 午前二時.

1984. Two P.M.   Gogo niji. 午後二時.

1985. It is exactly half-past three.   Chōdo sanji-han desu.
丁度三時半です.

1986. Quarter-past four.   Yoji jūgofun sugi.
四時十五分過ぎ.

1987. Quarter to five.   Goji jūgofun mae.
五時十五分前.

1988. At ten minutes to six.   Rokuji jippun mae ni.
六時十分前に。

1989. At twenty minutes past seven.
Shichiji nijippun sugi ni. 七時二十分過ぎに。

1990. It is early.   Hayai desu. 早いです。

1991. In the morning.   Asa. 朝。

1992. This morning.   Kesa. 今朝。

1993. This afternoon.   Kyō no gogo. 今日の午後。

1994. Evening.   Yūgata. 夕方。

1995. At noon.   Shōgo ni (OR: Ohiru ni).
正午に（お昼に）。

1996. At midnight.   Yoru jūniji ni. 夜十二時に。

1997. During the day.   Nitchū. 日中。

1998. Every day.   Mainichi. 毎日。

1999. Every night.   Maiban. 毎晩。

2000. All night.   Yodōshi. 夜通し。

2001. Since yesterday.   Kinō irai. 昨日以来。

2002. Today.   Kyō. 今日。

2003. Tomorrow.   Ashita (OR: Myōnichi). あした（明日）。

2004. Tonight. Kon-ya. 今夜。

2005. This evening. Komban. 今晩。

2006. Last month. Sengetsu. 先月。

2007. Next month. Raigetsu. 来月。

2008. This month. Kongetsu. 今月。

2009. This year. Kotoshi. 今年。

2010. Last year. Kyonen. 去年。

2011. Next year. Rainen. 来年。

2012. Next Sunday. Tsugi no nichiyōbi.
次の日曜日。

2013. Next week. Raishū. 来週。

2014. The day before yesterday. Issakujitsu (OR: Ototoi).
一昨日 (おとといい)。

2015. The day after tomorrow. Myōgonichi (OR: Asatte).
明後日 (あさって)。

2016. Two weeks ago. Nishūkan mae. 二週間前。

WEATHER

2017. How is the [weather] today?
Kyō no [otenki] wa dō desu ka?
今日の [お天気] はどうですか？

2018. It looks like rain. Ame no yō desu.
雨の様です。

2019. It is [cold]. [Samui] desu. [寒い] です。

2020. —fair. Hare—. 晴れ—。

2021. —warm. Atatakai—. 暖かい—。

2022. It is windy. Kaze ga fuite imasu.
風が吹いています。

2023. It is snowing. Yuki ga futte imasu.
雪が降っています。

2024. It is clearing up. Harete kimashita.
晴れて来ました。

2025. What a beautiful day! Nante ii otenki deshō!
何ていいお天気でしよう！

2026. I want to rest in the shade.
Hikage de yasumitai no desu. 日陰で休みたいのです。

2027. I want to sit in the sun. Hinatabokko o shitai no desu.
日向ぼっこをしたいのです。

2028. What is the weather forecast for [tomorrow] [the weekend]?
[Ashita] [Shūmatsu] no tenki yohō wa?
[明日][週末]の天気予報は？

2029. There will be snow tomorrow.
Myōnichi wa yuki desu. 明日は雪です。

DAYS OF THE WEEK

2030. Sunday. Nichiyōbi. 日曜日。

2031. Monday. Getsuyōbi. 月曜日。

2032. Tuesday. Kayōbi. 火曜日。

2033. Wednesday. Suiyōbi. 水曜日。

2034. Thursday. Mokuyōbi. 木曜日。

2035. Friday. Kin-yōbi. 金曜日。

2036. Saturday. Doyōbi. 土曜日。

HOLIDAYS

2037. A public holiday. Ippan kōkyūbi. 一般公休日。

2038. [Merry] Christmas. [Merī] Kurisumasu.
[メリー] クリスマス。

2039. Happy New Year! Akemashite omedetō!
明けましておめでとう！

2040. New Year's. Oshōgatsu (OR: Ganjitsu).
お正月（元日）。

2041. New Year's Eve. Ōmisoka. 大晦日。

2042. Empire Day (Feb. 11). Kenkokusai. 建国祭。

2043. Constitution Day (May 3). Kempō kinembi.
憲法記念日。

2044. Children's Day (May 5). Kodomo no hi.
子供の日。

2045. Lantern Festival (mid-July).
Bon matsuri (OR: Obon).
盆祭リ（お盆）。

DATES, MONTHS AND SEASONS

2046. January. Ichigatsu. 一月。

2047. February. Nigatsu. 二月。

2048. March. Sangatsu. 三月。

2049. April. Shigatsu. 四月。

2050. May. Gogatsu. 五月。

2051. June. Rokugatsu. 六月。

2052. July. Shichigatsu. 七月。

2053. August. Hachigatsu. 八月。

2054. September. Kugatsu. 九月。

2055. October. Jūgatsu. 十月。

2056. November. Jūichigatsu. 十一月。

2057. December. Jūnigatsu. 十二月。

2058. The spring. Haru. 春。

2059. The summer. Natsu. 夏 .

2060. The autumn. Aki. 秋 。

2061. The winter. Fuyu. 冬 。

2062. Today is the 31st of May, [1983].
Kyō wa [sen-kyūhyaku hachijūsannen] gogatsu
   sanjūichinichi desu.
今日は[千九百八十三年]五月三十一日です。

NUMBERS: CARDINALS*

2063. Zero. Rei (J.: Zero). 零（ゼロ）。

2064. One. Ichi (J.: Hitotsu). 一（一つ）。

2065. Two. Ni (J.: Futatsu). 二（二つ）。

2066. Three. San (J.: Mittsu). 三（三つ）。

2067. Four. Shi (J.: Yottsu). 四（四つ）。

2068. Five. Go (J.: Itsutsu). 五（五つ）。

2069. Six. Roku (J.: Muttsu). 六（六つ）。

2070. Seven. Shichi (J.: Nanatsu). 七（七つ）。

---

* The Japanese number system is extremely complex. There are two
sets of numbers for counting up to 10, one Chinese and the other
native Japanese (J.). The numbers above 10 are formed from the
borrowed Chinese words only. Numbers are usually used together
with "counting words," which vary according to what is counted and
often undergo phonetic changes depending on the number they combine
with.

2071. Eight. Hachi (J.: Yattsu). 八 (八つ).

2072. Nine. Ku (J.: Kokonotsu). 九 (九つ).

2073. Ten. Jū (J.: Tō). 十 (十).

2074. Eleven. Jūichi. 十一.

2075. Twelve. Jūni. 十二.

2076. Thirteen. Jūsan. 十三.

2077. Fourteen. Jūshi (OR: Jūyon). 十四.

2078. Fifteen. Jūgo. 十五.

2079. Sixteen. Jūroku. 十六.

2080. Seventeen. Jūshichi. 十七.

2081. Eighteen. Jūhachi. 十八.

2082. Nineteen. Jūku. 十九.

2083. Twenty. Nijū. 二十.

2084. Twenty-one. Nijū-ichi. 二十一.

2085. Twenty-five. Nijū-go. 二十五.

2086. Thirty. Sanjū. 三十.

2087. Forty. Yonjū (OR: Shijū). 四十.

2088. Fifty. Gojū. 五十.

2089. Sixty. Rokujū. 六十。

2090. Seventy. Shichijū (OR: Nanajū).
七十。

2091. Eighty. Hachijū. 八十。

2092. Ninety. Kujū (OR: Kyūjū). 九十。

2093. One hundred. Hyaku. 百。

2094. One hundred one. Hyaku-ichi. 百一。

2095. One hundred ten. Hyaku-jū. 百十。

2096. One thousand. Sen (OR: Issen). 千 (一千)。

2097. Two thousand. Nisen. 二千。

2098. Three thousand. Sanzen. 三千。

2099. Four thousand. Yonsen. 四千。

2100. Five thousand. Gosen. 五千。

2101. Ten thousand. Ichiman. 一万。

2102. One hundred thousand. Jūman. 十万。

2103. One million. Hyakuman. 百万。

NUMBERS: ORDINALS

2104. The first. Dai-ichi. 第一。

2105. The second.   Dai-ni. 第二。

2106. The third.   Dai-san. 第三。

2107. The fourth.   Dai-yon. 第四。

2108. The fifth.   Dai-go. 第五。

2109. The sixth.   Dai-roku. 第六。

2110. The seventh.   Dai-shichi. 第七。

2111. The eighth.   Dai-hachi. 第八。

2112. The ninth.   Dai-ku. 第九。

2113. The tenth.   Dai-jū. 第十。

2114. The twentieth.   Dai-nijū. 第二十。

2115. The thirtieth.   Dai-sanjū. 第三十。

2116. The hundredth.   Dai-hyaku. 第百。

2117. The thousandth.   Dai-issen. 第一千。

QUANTITIES

2118. A fraction.   Bunsū. 分数。

2119. One-quarter.   Yombun no ichi. 四分の一。

2120. One-third.   Sambun no ichi. 三分の一。

2121. One-half. Hambun (OR: Nibun no ichi).
半分（二分の一）。

2122. Three-quarters. Yombun no san. 四分の三。

2123. The whole. Zentai (OR: Zembu).
全体（全部）。

2124. A pair. Ittsui. 一対。

2125. A dozen. Ichi dāsu. 一ダース。

2126. Half a dozen. Han dāsu. 半ダース。

2127. A few. Shōsū. 少数。

2128. Several. Kazukazu no (OR: Ikutsuka).
数々の（いくつか）。

2129. Many. Takusan. 沢山。

FAMILY

2130. Wife (one's own).* Kanai. 家内。

2131. Wife (another's).* Okusan. 奥さん。

2132. Husband (one's own). Shujin. 主人。

2133. Husband (another's). Goshujin. 御主人。

---

* When you refer to someone else's relations, you express respect by using a different vocabulary than when referring to your own relations.

2134. Mother (one's own). Haha. 母 。

2135. Mother (another's). Okāsan. お母さん。

2136. Father (one's own). Chichi. 父 。

2137. Father (another's). Otōsan. お父さん。

2138. Grandmother (one's own). Sobo. 祖母 。

2139. Grandmother (another's). Obāsan. お婆さん。

2140. Grandfather (one's own). Sofu. 祖父 。

2141. Grandfather (another's). Ojiisan. おじいさん。

2142. Daughter (one's own). Musume. 娘 。

2143. Daughter (another's). Ojōsan. お嬢さん。

2144. Son (one's own). Musuko. 息子 。

2145. Son (another's). Musukosan. 息子さん。

2146. [Younger] [Older] sister (one's own).
[Imōto] [Ane]. 〔妹 〕〔姉〕 。

2147. [Younger] [Older] sister (another's).
[Imōtosan] [Onēsan]. 〔妹さん〕〔お姉さん〕 。

2148. [Younger] [Older] brother (one's own).
[Otōto] [Ani]. 〔弟〕〔兄〕 。

2149. [Younger] [Older] brother (another's).
[Otōtosan] [Oniisan]. 〔弟さん〕〔お兄さん〕 。

2150. Relative.   Shinseki.   親戚。

2151. Adults.   Otona.   大人。

2152. Children.   Kodomo.   子供。

COMMON SIGNS & PUBLIC NOTICES

2153. Admission.   Nyūjōryō.   入場料。

2154. Admission free.   Nyūjō muryō.   入場無料。

2155. Air-conditioned.   Reibō sōchi ari (OR: Kūrā-tsuki).
冷房装置あり（クーラー付き）。

2156. Arrival.   Tōchaku.   到着。

2157. Attention.   Chūi.   注意。

2158. Bargain.   Tokubai (OR: Sēru).   特売（セール）。

2159. Bathing not allowed.   Suiyoku o kinzu.
水浴を禁ず。

2160. Beware of dog.   Mōken ari, chūi. 猛犬あり、注意。

2161. Bus stop.   Basu teiryūjo. バス停留所。

2162. Business school.   Shōgyō gakkō. 商業学校。

2163. Cemetery.   Bochi. 墓地。

2164. City hall.   Shiyakusho. 市役所。

2165. Clinic.   Gairai kanja shinsatsujo.
外来患者診察所。

2166. Closed.   Kyūgyō. 休業。

2167. Closed from 8 P.M. to 9 A.M.
Gogo hachiji kara gozen kuji made heiten.
午後八時から午前九時まで閉店。

2168. Closed on Sundays and holidays.
Nichiyō saijitsu kyūgyō. 日曜祭日休業。

2169. Continuous performance.   Renzoku kōgyō.
連続興行。

2170. Danger.   Kiken. 危険。

2171. Departure (train).   Hassha. 発車。

2172. Dining car.   Shokudōsha. 食堂車。

2173. Dining room.   Shokudō. 食堂。

2174. Do not feed the animals.
Dōbutsu ni tabemono o ataenai koto.
動物に食べ物を与えないこと。

2175. Doorkeeper (OR: Doorman).
Genkamban (OR: Mon-ei). 玄関番 (門衛)。

2176. Down.   Shita. 下。

2177. Elevator.   Erebētā. エレベーター。

2178. Emergency exit.   Hijōguchi. 非常口。

2179. Employees only. Jūgyōin-yō. 従業員用.

2180. Engaged (OR: **Occupied**). Shiyōchū. 使用中.

2181. Entrance. Iriguchi. 入口.

2182. Escalator. Esukarētā. エスカレーター.

2183. Exit. Deguchi. 出口.

2184. Forbidden. Genkin. 厳禁.

2185. For sale. Urimono. 売り物.

2186. For hire (taxi). Haiyā. ハイヤー.

2187. Free. Muryō. 無料.

2188. Fresh paint. Penki nuritate. ペンキ塗り立て.

2189. Furnished rooms for rent.
Kagutsuki kashishitsu ari. 家具付き貸し室あり.

2190. Gentlemen (OR: **Men's room**). Danshiyō benjo.
男子用便所.

2191. Hospital. Byōin. 病院.

2192. House for rent. Kashiya. 貸家.

2193. Imperial gardens. Gyoen. 御苑.

2194. Information. Annaijo. 案内所.

2195. Keep off the grass. Shibafu ni tachiiru bekarazu.
芝生に立ち入る可からず.

2196. Ladies (OR: **Ladies' room**).   Joshiyō benjo.
女子用便所。

2197. Lunch.   Chūshoku. 昼食。

2198. Men (OR: **Men's room**).   Danshiyō benjo.
男子用便所。

2199. Men at work (construction).   Kōjichū. 工事中。

2200. No admittance.   Nyūjō shazetsu. 入場謝絶。

2201. No admittance except on business.
Muyō no mono iru bekarazu. 無用の者入る可からず。

2202. No noise.   Oshizuka ni. お静かに。

2203. No smoking.   Kin-en. 禁煙。

2204. No spitting.   Tantsuba o haku bekarazu.
たんつばを吐く可からず。

2205. No swimming.   Oyogi o kinzu. 泳ぎを禁ず。

2206. No trespassing.   Tōrinuke muyō. 通り抜け無用。

2207. Occupied.   Shiyōchū. 使用中。

2208. On sale now.   Hambaichū. 販売中。

2209. Open for business.   Eigyōchū. 営業中。

2210. Open from 9 A.M. to 8 P.M.
Eigyō jikan: gozen kuji kara gogo hachiji.
営業時間:午前九時から午後八時。

2211. Open nights.   Yakan eigyō. 夜間営業。

2212. Park (public).   Kōen. 公園。

2213. Pedestrians only.   Hokōsha yō. 歩行者用。

2214. Police.   Keikan (OR: Junsa). 警官 (巡査)。

2215. Police box.   Kōban. 交番。

2216. Police station.   Keisatsu. 警察。

2217. Post no bills.   Harigami muyō. はり紙無用。

2218. Private property.   Shiyū. 私有。

2219. Private road.   Shidō. 私道。

2220. Public lavatory.   Kōshū benjo. 公衆便所。

2221. Public scribe.   Daisho. 代書。

2222. Public telephone.   Kōshū denwa. 公衆電話。

2223. Pull.   Hiku. 引く。

2224. Push.   Osu. 押す。

2225. Quiet.   Oshizuka ni. お静かに。

2226. Railroad station.   Sutēshon (OR: Eki).
ステーション (駅)。

2227. Refreshments.   Chaka. 茶菓。

2228. Reserved.   Yoyakuzumi. 予約済み。

2229. Retail. Kouri. 小売 。

2230. Ring the bell (OR: **buzzer**).
Beru (OR: Buzā) o narashite kudasai.
ベル(ブザー)を鳴らして下さい。

2231. Sale. Uridashi. 売出し 。

2232. Self-service. Serufu sābisu. セルフ・サービス 。

2233. Silence. Chimmoku. 沈黙 。

2234. Silence (for prayer). Mokutō. 黙とう 。

2235. Smoking car. Kitsuensha. 喫煙車 。

2236. Smoking room. Kitsuenshitsu. 喫煙室 。

2237. Sold. Baiyakuzumi. 売約済み 。

2238. Sold out. Urikire. 売り切れ 。

2239. Stairs. Kaidan. 階段 。

2240. Taxi stand. Takushī. タクシー 。

2241. Ticket gate. Kaisatsuguchi. 改札口 。

2242. Ticket office. Kippu uriba. 切符売場 。

2243. To the trains. Jōshaguchi. 乗車口 。

2244. Toilet. Toire (OR: Otoire; OR: Otearai; OR: Benjo).
トイレ(おトイレ; お手洗い; 便所) 。

2245. Up. Ue. 上 。

2246. Vacant (taxi).   Kūsha. 空車。

2247. Vacant (house).   Akiya. 空き家。

2248. Waiting room.   Machiaishitsu. 待合室。

2249. Warning.   Chūi. 注意。

2250. Watch your step.   Ashimoto ni goyōjin.
足もとに御用心。

2251. Wholesale.   Oroshiuri. 卸し売り。

2252. Will return at [1 P.M.].   [Gogo ichiji] ni modorimasu.
[午後一時]に戻ります。

2253. Year-end sale.   Seibo uridashi. 歳暮売出し。

2254. Zoo.   Dōbutsuen. 動物園。

INDEX

The words, phrases and sentences in this book are numbered consecutively from 1 to 2254, and the entries in this index refer to those numbers. In addition, major section headings (capitalized entries) refer to the page number on which the section begins. The abbreviations *adj.* for adjective, *adv.* for adverb, *n.* for noun, and *v.* for verb indicate parts of speech (where there may be confusion). J. stands for Japanese; often Japanese and Western versions of the same thing (an umbrella, for example) have different names. Parentheses are used for explanations, to enclose optional portions of a Japanese phrase, and to mark the "honorific particles" *o* and *go*, which are used with many words to express respect.

Every English word in the index is followed by one or more Japanese equivalents, generally given in dictionary form. The reader is thereby provided with a basic, up-to-date English-Japanese glossary. Of course, an acquaintance with Japanese grammar is necessary for making the best use of this index, especially since Japanese grammar and Japanese idioms are very different from those of other languages. The correspondence between an English entry and its Japanese equivalent is therefore sometimes inexact. While the names of everyday objects are relatively unambiguous and straightforward, verbs especially often depend on context for their meaning to be clear. Always refer back to the numbered sentences for more information. For those words (adjectives, adverbs and verbs) that take more than one form, the index lists not only their first appearance, but all entries in which the basic form is significantly altered. For example, under "leave," two forms are listed for the Japanese verb *deru: demasu* (the polite present) in phrase 60, and *demashō* (the polite probable) in phrase 1133.

Because of the already large extent of the indexed material, invariable words have been listed only once, and only one example of each form found in the book has been included in the index. Cross-indexing has generally been avoided, and phrases of two or more words will usually be found under only one of their components. If you do not find a phrase listed under one word, try another. When a numbered sentence contains a choice of Japanese equivalents, usually only the first choice has been included in the index.

When more than one Japanese word is listed for an English entry, the beginner will find it helpful to look at all the phrases given, in order to gain some idea of the range of variations and shades of meaning for the words listed. It is not the purpose of this volume to give all the possible grammatical variations and nuances of meaning; you will need a Japanese grammar and dictionary for that. The index will, however, give you the proper form to look up in a dictionary or grammar, where you will find further information.

bell: *beru* 2230
bellhop: *bōi-san* 617
belly: *onaka* 1914
belt: *bando* 1358
beside: *waki* 229
best: *ichiban ii* 557
better: *mō sukoshi ii* 1293
BEVERAGES AND
   BREAKFAST FOODS,
   p. 71
beware of dog: *mōken ari,
   chūi* 2160
beyond: *saki* 218
bib: *yodarekake* 1789
bicarbonate of soda:
   jūtansan sōda 1517
bicycle: *jitensha* 369
big: *ōkii* 1312
bill (*n.*, banknote): *satsu*
   1270; (check): *kanjō* 630;
   kanjōgaki 1347; (*v.*):
   tsuke ni suru 537
birthday: *tanjōbi* 46
bitten, be (insect): *sasareru*
   1840
black: *kuro* 179, 1418
black-and-white: *kuro
   shiro* 1594
blanket: *mōfu* 642
bleed: *shukketsu suru* 1901
blister: *mizubukure* 1841
blood: *chi* 1915; — vessel:
   kekkan 1916
blouse: *burausu* 1357
blowfish: *fugu* 908

blue: *ao* 1419
board (*v.*): *norikomu* 287;
   go on — (boat): *jōsen
   suru* 245
boarding: — house:
   geshukuya 559; — pass:
   norikomi ken 295
BOAT, p. 22
bobby pin: *bobi pin* 1518
body: *karada* 1917
boiled (food): *nitamono* 787
bolt: *boruto* 420
bone: *hone* 1918
bonito, dried: *katsuobushi*
   824; — shavings:
   hanagatsuo 825
bon voyage: *gobuji de itte
   irasshai* 246
book (*n.*): *hon* 1464; (*v.*):
   yoyaku suru 1097
bookshop: *hon-ya* 1719
BOOKSHOP,
   STATIONER AND
   NEWSDEALER, p. 115
boot: *būtsu* 1359
bored, I am: *taikutsu desu*
   1128
boric acid: *hōsan* 1519
bother, don't: *dōzo okamai
   naku* 17
bottle (baby): *gyūnyūki*
   1780
Bourbon whiskey: *burubon
   uisuki* 721
bowling: *bōringu* 1217

exchange): *ryōgae* 1261;
(= small change): *tsuri*
351; (= transfer):
norikae 331; (v.): *kaeru*
394; (= exchange)
torikaeru 643
character (J.): *kanji* 128
charge (v., battery): *jūden
suru* 402; person in —:
kakari no mono 137;
reverse the —s:
sempōbarai ni suru 536;
what is the —: *ikura desu
ka* 535
chassis: *shadai* 425
cheap: *yasui* 1288
cheaper: *mō sukoshi yasui*
593
check (n.): *kogitte* 1264;
(bill): *(o)kanjō* 815; (tire
· pressure): *hakaru* 405
checkers: *chekkā* 1219
check-out (n.): *chekku auto*
628
checkroom: *azukarijo* 1722
cheek: *hō* 1922
cheers (toast): *kampai* 734
cherry: *sakurambo* 981
chess: *chesu* 1218; (J.): *go*
1220
chest (body): *mune* 1923;
(drawers): *tansu* 673
chestnuts: *kuri* 982
chewing gum: *chūingamu*
1520

chicken (food): *toriniku*
900; — and egg with
rice: *oyako domburi*
1055; — balls: *toriganni*
1032; — broiled on
skewers: *yakitori* 1022;
— liver: *kimo* 901;
— soup: *chikin sūpu* 878
chicken pox: *mizubōsō*
1844
child: *kodomo* 2152
children's: — day: *kodomo
no hi* 2044; — dresses:
kodomo no doresu 1370
chill (bodily): *samuke* 1845
chin: *ago* 1924
china: *setomono* 1454
chives: *nira* 822
chocolate: *chokorēto* 1003;
hot —: *hotto kokoa* 856
choke (n.): *chōku* 426
chopped (food):
kizandamono 789;
— flavorings: *yakumi*
823
chopsticks: *(o)hashi* 772;
disposable —:
waribashi 773
Christmas, Merry: *merī
Kurisumasu* 2038
chrysanthemum leaves:
shungiku 948
church: *kyōkai* 1138
cigar: *hamaki* 1639
cigarette: *tabako* 1640

hardware store: *kanamonoya* 1741

hat: *bōshi* 1273; — shop: *bōshiya* 1742

hay fever: *kafunshō* 1858

he: *kare* 94

head: *atama* 1942

headache: *zutsū* 1860

headlight: *heddo raito* 464

health: *kenkō* 159; — certificate: *kenkō shōmeisho* 159

HEALTH AND ILLNESS, p. 139

hear: *kikoeru* 546, 1170

hearing aid: *hochōki* 1671

heart: *shinzō* 1943

heater: *hītā* 366

heavier (texture): *mō sukoshi atsubottai* 1298

heel: *kakato* 1670

height: *takasa* 1317

hello: *konnichi wa* 1; (on phone): *moshimoshi* 540

help (v.): *tasukeru* 151; *te o kasu* 391; can you — me: *onegai dekimasu ka* 138; please — me: *chotto onegai shimasu* 139

here: *koko* 23

herring: *nishin* 915; — roe: *kazu no ko* 830

high chair: *bebīyō isu* 1791

higher: *mō sukoshi ue* 596

hike: *haiku* 1245

hill: *saka* 233

hip: *koshi* 1945

hire, for: *haiyā* 2186

hold (v., mail): *hokan suru* 522

holiday: *kōkyūbi* 2037; *saijitsu* 2168

HOLIDAYS, p. 155

home: *otaku* 1795; (one's own): *jitaku* 537

hood: *fuddo* 454

horn (auto): *hōn* 455

horseback riding: *umanori* 1231

horsepower: *bariki* 456

horse races: *keiba* 1225

horseradish (J.): *wasabi* 832

hospital: *byōin* 1795

hostel: *hosuteru* 1235

hot: *atsui* 100, 637

hotcakes: *hottokēki* 870

HOTEL, p. 48

hotel: *hoteru* 225

HOTEL STAFF, p. 55

hot-water bottle: *yutampo* 1547

hour, per: *ichi jikan* 338

house for rent: *kashiya* 2192

housemaid: *jochū* 690

housewares: *zakkaten* 1743

how: *dō* 68; — are things: *dō desu ka* 41; — are you: *ikaga desu ka* 38; — do you do it: *dō suru*

mother (another's): *okāsan* 2135; (one's own): *haha* 2134

motor: *mōtā* 409

motorcycle: *ōtobai* 370

mountain: *yama* 1100

mouth: *kuchi* 1956

mouthwash: *kuchiyusugi* 1554

move (*v.*): *ugokasu* 1900

movies: *eiga* 1182

Mr.: *San* 36

Mrs.: *San* 36

mud: *nukarumi* 395

muffler: *mafurā* 471

mumps: *otafukukaze* 1867

muscle: *kinniku* 1851

museum: *hakubutsukan* 1121

mushroom: *masshurūmu* 953; (J.): *matsutake* 955; dried —: *shiitake* 954

music: *ongaku* 1139; — store: *gakkiten* 1753

musical: — comedy: *myūjikaru komedi* 1183; — instruments: *gakki* 1754

mustache: *kuchihige* 1692

mustard: *karashi* 839; — greens: *karashina* 956

mutton: *yōniku* 895

my: *watakushi no* 156

nail (finger): *te no tsume* 1934; (metal): *kugi* 472; — file: *tsume no yasuri* 1555; — polish: *tsume migaki* 1556

name: (*o*)*namae* 84

nap: *hirune* 1783

napkin: *nafukin* 759

nausea: *hakike* 1868

navel: *heso* 1958

near: *chikai* 207

nearest: *ichiban chikai* 324

neck: *kubi* 1959

necklace: *nekkuresu* 168

necktie: *nekutai* 1383

need (*v.*): *iru* 1227

needle: *nuibari* 1678

negative (*n.*): *nega* 1605

nerve: *shinkei* 1960

neutral gear: *nūtoraru* 449

new: *atarashii* 1321

newspaper: *shimbun* 1474

newsstand: *shimbun baiten* 1755

New Year('s): (*o*)*shōgatsu* 2040; — Eve: *ōmisoka* 2041; Happy —: *akemashite omedetō* 2039

New York: *Nyū Yōku* 528

next: *tsugi no* 213; — week: *raishū* 50

night: all —: *yodōshi* 368; every —: *maiban* 1999; for one —: *hitoban* 580; — letter: *yakan kansō*

opera: *opera* 1186;
— glasses: *opera gurasu* 1187

opposite (*preposition*): *no mukai* 228

orange (color): *orenji iro* 1425; (fruit): *orenji* 860

orchestra seat: *ikkai seki* 1165

order (n.): *chūmon* 1313; (v.): *chūmon suru* 811; in —: *totonotte* 362

orlon: *oruron* 1447

orthopedist: *seikeigeka-i* 1830

other, the: *achira* 215

outdoors: *soto* 747

over: *no ue* 236

overheat: *ōbā hīto* 409

overnight: *hitoban* 380

oysters: *kaki* 919

pacifier: *oshaburi* 1784

pack (v.): *hōsō suru* 1346

package (n.): *kozutsumi* 176; *tsutsumi* 514

pageboy: *pēji-san* 620

pail: *baketsu* 696

pain: *itami* 1799

pain-killer: *chintsūzai* 1504

paint (artist's): *enogu* 1757; (house): *penki* 1758; fresh —: *penki nuritate* 2188

painted screen: *byōbu* 1624

painting (art): *kaiga* 1112

pair: *ittsui* 2124

pajamas: *pajama* 1385

palace: *goten* 1119

palm (hand): *tenohira* 1962

pancake: *pankēki* 869

pancreas: *suizō* 1963

panties: *pantī* 1386

paper: *yōshi* 1479

papers (documents): *shorui* 362

parcel: *kozutsumi* 615;
— post: *kozutsumi yūbin* 512

pardon (me): *shitsurei* 54

park (n.): *kōen* 228

parking lot: *chūshajō* 387

part (v., hair): *wakeru* 1688

PARTS OF THE BODY, p. 147

PARTS OF THE CAR AND AUTO EQUIPMENT, p. 37

passport: *pasupōto* 144

pastry: *yōgashi* 1002;
— shop: *yōgashiya* 1759

paved: *hōsō shita* 376

pay (v.): *harau* 1336, 1341, 1349

peach: *momo* 991

pear: *nashi* 992

pearl: *shinju* 1625

peas: *endōmame* 959

pedal: *pedaru* 475

tent: *tento* 1251
tenth: *dai-jū* 2113
terrace: *terasu* 704
textiles: *orimonorui* 1441
thanks: *arigatō* 13
that (*adj.*): *ano* 77; (*pron.*):
  are 182; *sore* 55; — way:
  achira no hoko 212
theater: *gekijō* 1192;
  movie —: *eigakan* 1193
thermometer: *taionkei*
  1586
thermos: *mahōbin* 1252
these: *kono* 626
thief: *dorobō* 152
thigh: *futo momo* 1974
thimble: *yubinuki* 1679
thing: *mono* 174
think: *omou* 123
third (*adj.*): *dai-san* 2106;
  (*n.*): *sambun no ichi* 2120;
  — gear: *sādo* 446
thirsty: *nodo ga kawaku*
  102
thirteen: *jūsan* 2076
thirtieth: *dai-sanjū* 2115
thirty: *sanjū* 2086
thirty-five: *sanjūgo* 1596
thirty-six: *sanjūroku* 1313
this: *kore* 55
thousand: *sen* 2096
thousandth: *dai-issen*
  2117
thread: *nui-ito* 1680
three: *san* 2066; (persons):

  sannin 742; — thousand:
  sanzen 2098
throat: *nodo* 1975
thumb: *oyayubi* 1976
Thursday: *mokuyōbi* 2034
ticket: *ken* 1169; — gate:
  kaisatsuguchi 314;
  — office: *kippu uriba*
  2242; *shussatsuguchi*
  297; — stub: *ken no*
  hikae 1169
tighter: *mō sukoshi kitsuku*
  1300
TIME, p. 151
time: *jikan* 304; on —:
  jikan dōri 280; *yotei dōri*
  292; what —: *nanji* 271
timetable: *jikokuhyō* 302
tip (= gratuity): *chippu*
  189
tire: *taiya* 394; — pressure:
  taiya no puresshā 405;
  — pump: *kūki ire* 495;
  spare —: *supeya taiya*
  493
tired, I am: *tsukaremashita*
  105
toast: *tōsuto* 864
tobacco: *tabako* 1650;
  — pouch: *paipu tabako*
  ire 1651; — store:
  tabakoya 1638
TOBACCO STORE, p.
  126
today: *kyō* 518

APPENDIX:
COMMON ROAD SIGNS

Migi kāvu.
Right bend.

Jūjiro.
Intersection.

U setsu.
Right turn.

Kodomo ni chūi.
Children.

Fumikiri.
Railroad crossing.

T-gata kōsa.
T intersection.

Surippu ni chūi.
Slippery when wet.

Kudarizaka chūi.
Hill.

Dōro kōjichū.
Construction.

Kiken.
Danger.

Tomare.
Stop.

Jokō.
Slow down.

Oikoshi kinshi.
No passing.

Saikō sokudo.
Maximum speed.

Saitei sokudo.
Minimum speed.

Chūsha teisha kinshi.
No parking or stopping.

Chūsha kinshi.
No parking.

Tsūkōdome.
No entry.

Norimono kinshi.
Closed to all vehicles.

Ōtobai sen-yō.
Closed to all vehicles except
motorcycles.

国道
ROUTE

Kokudō.
National highway.

Kendō.
Prefectural highway.

Basu sen-yō.
Bus lane.

Chūsha.
Parking permitted.

Teisha.
Stopping permitted.

Ōdan kinshi.
Crossing by pedestrians prohibited.

Hokōsha ōdan.
Pedestrian crossing.

Hokōsha jitensha sen-yō.
Pedestrians and bicycles only.

Basu sen-yō.
Buses only.

Hokōsha sen-yō.
Pedestrians only.

Deguchi.
Exit.

LISTEN & LEARN CASSETTES

Complete, practical at-home language learning courses for people with limited study time—specially designed for travelers.

Special features:

* Dual-language—Each phrase first in English, then the foreign-language equivalent, followed by a pause for repetition (allows for easy use of cassette even without manual).

* Native speakers—Spoken by natives of the country who are language teachers at leading colleges and universities.

* Convenient manual—Contains every word on the cassettes—all fully indexed for fast phrase or word location.

Each boxed set contains one 90-minute cassette and complete manual.

Precise, to-the-point guides for adults with limited learning time

ESSENTIAL GRAMMAR SERIES

Designed for independent study or as supplements to conventional courses, the *Essential Grammar* series provides clear explanations of all aspects of grammar—no trivia, no archaic material. Do not confuse these volumes with abridged grammars. These volumes are complete.

ESSENTIAL FRENCH GRAMMAR, Seymour Resnick. Includes 2500 item cognate list. 159pp. 5⅜ × 8½. •20419-7 Pa. $2.75

ESSENTIAL GERMAN GRAMMAR, Guy Stern and E. F. Bleiler. Unusual shortcuts on noun declension, word order. 124pp. 5⅜ × 8½. •20422-7 Pa. $2.95

ESSENTIAL ITALIAN GRAMMAR, Olga Ragusa. Includes useful discussion of verb idioms essential in Italian. 111pp. 5⅜ × 8½. •20779-X Pa. $2.95

ESSENTIAL JAPANESE GRAMMAR, E. F. Bleiler. In Romaji, no characters needed. Japanese grammar is regular and simple. 156pp. 5⅜ × 8½. 21027-8 Pa. $2.95

ESSENTIAL PORTUGUESE GRAMMAR, Alexander da R. Prista. Includes 4 appendices covering regular, irregular verbs. 114pp. 5⅜ × 8½. 21650-0 Pa. $3.50

ESSENTIAL SPANISH GRAMMAR, Seymour Resnick. Includes 2500 word cognate list. 115pp. 5⅜ × 8½. •20780-3 Pa. $2.75

ESSENTIAL ENGLISH GRAMMAR, Philip Gucker. Combines modern functional and traditional approaches. 177pp. 5⅜ × 8½. 21649-7 Pa. $3.50

•Not available in British Commonwealth Countries except Canada.